Family Literacy:

Bury College
Enterprise LRC

• BURY •
COLLEGE

Basic Skills
Agency

Acknowledgements

The project team is particularly grateful for the co-operation, help and generous hospitality provided by the staff and students of the 18 family literacy programmes involved in our research, in the following areas:

Birmingham, Bodmin, Brighton, Cleveland, Coventry, Lewisham, Rhondda Fach, Rochdale, Sheffield, Swansea, Swindon, Worthing. We should also like to thank Basic Skills Agency staff; school and Local Education Authority staff in the areas which we visited; and the staff of small grants programmes in Leeds and Billingham.

We are also grateful to the following people for their support and help during the project: members of the project Steering Group, and in particular, Professor Hazel Francis and Graham Frater; Professor Martin Hughes, Anita Davidson, Sue Lumb, Mary MacMullen and Julie Williams.

© The Basic Skills Agency
Commonwealth House, 1-19 New Oxford Street, London WC1A 1NU.

Published May 1997

ISBN 1 85990 064 X

Design: Studio 21

Contents

Foreword

A MAJOR part of the initiatives we undertook to develop family literacy was the funding, through a programme of small grants, of local innovation. These small grants – and we gave over four hundred between November 1993 and March 1997 – provided opportunities for parents to improve and strengthen reading and writing skills. Just as importantly, it gave them the chance to work with their children to make sure they got a good start with literacy. The grants were modest, averaging £1839.34 and they had to be matched by hard pressed local funding.

A wide variety of approaches were used to develop family literacy programmes with the help of our small grants. Not all of these worked effectively; after all programmes were targeted at people who had little to feel grateful for from an education system that had not seemed to serve them very well.

Whether innovation works or not, I think it's important to make sure the lessons from local work don't just stay local. This independent evaluative report from Exeter University draws out the practice that developed in a sample of eighteen of the programmes we supported and provides examples of effectiveness that will be important for the further development of family literacy.

It's not, of course, the same as objective research based on the assessment of parents and their children's literacy skills. The NFER research into the effectiveness of the four Demonstration Programmes we also funded provides that necessary objective research. What this report does is provide a useful source of ideas about practice that should be helpful for anyone running, or thinking of setting up, a family literacy programme.

Alan Wells OBE
Director

CHAPTER ONE

Why Family Literacy?

THERE is considerable evidence to suggest that when parents have difficulties in reading, writing and other basic skills, their children are likely to experience similar difficulties and are less likely to be able to benefit from the educational opportunities available (e.g. research commissioned by the Basic Skills Agency, based on the fifth sweep of the National Child Development Study, (ALBSU, 1993)) and research in the USA (e.g. National Assessment of Educational Progress, 1991; Sticht, Beller & McDonald, 1992).

Until recently, many of the initiatives and interventions which aimed to address the link between parents' and children's achievements in literacy focused on providing programmes for either adults or children. However, adult education programmes and parenting courses do not necessarily have a direct impact on children; nor do programmes providing extra support for children in literacy learning address the connection between parents and children's achievement. The beneficial impact of parents' participation in adult education may be realised only in the medium or long term. This would have little immediate effect on the critical early phase of young children's development and schooling. Many adults want to improve their basic skills in order to be able to support their children's literacy learning. However, the connection between adults improving their own basic skills and supporting their children in literacy is not always obvious. Ryan, Geisler and Knell (1994) have shown that parents who are potential recruits to family literacy programmes do not necessarily perceive their own educational goals – such as getting more qualifications or learning new skills – as directly relevant to improving their families' lives.

More recently, work in the USA (e.g. St Pierre et al. 1994) has indicated that a better approach to this problem may be to provide opportunities for parents and children to learn together. This approach tackles directly the inter-generational effect of under-achievement in literacy.

For example, an important step in addressing the inter-generational link between parents' and children's achievement in literacy is to help parents to identify their role as their child's educational advocate.

Family literacy is used to describe many different types of provision. The National Foundation of Educational Research (NFER) evaluation of the Family Literacy Demonstration Programmes has already indicated the range of meanings accorded to the term *family literacy* (Brooks et al., 1996). For example, there are already numerous schemes to encourage parental involvement in children's literacy at school. It is well known that parental support/encouragement and a literacy-aware home environment can help children in their literacy development (e.g. Tizard, Schofield & Hewison, 1982; Topping & Wolfendale, 1985). However, Francis (1994) and Hannon (1995) both suggest that existing parental involvement programmes have tended to concentrate on reading. The emphasis has also been on parents supporting children's literacy in school, rather than helping parents to realise how everyday home events also may support children's literacy development.

Parents with low basic skills are less likely to take part in parental involvement schemes. Where they do take part, they are often not in a position to take full advantage of what is on offer. Thus there needs to be support for parents with low basic skills which makes explicit links with how parents can support children's literacy learning at home and school.

Family literacy may build upon and extend previous work with parents such as schemes for parental involvement in children's reading; it is intended to complement rather than duplicate or replace other forms of provision. What is distinctive about the approach of the Basic Skills Agency to family literacy, is that it deliberately sets out to address the inter-generational link between parents' and children's achievement in literacy. It does so by ensuring that provision is made for children and for adults in their own right, and for children and adults to work together. It is in this respect that family literacy differs from other forms of provision which aim to help parents with basic skills, or support children with learning difficulties, or involve parents in supporting their children in school work.

The Basic Skills Agency's Family Literacy Initiative

The Basic Skills Agency began its initiative in family literacy in 1993. It included four large-scale demonstration programmes in four areas of

England and Wales, promotional work, the production of materials for teachers and a small grants programme. In addition, research was commissioned into both the demonstration and the small grants programmes. The work undertaken in the four large-scale demonstration programmes is described in detail in the evaluative study undertaken by the NFER (Brooks et al., 1996). The subject of the research described in this report was the small grants programme.

Through the small grants programme, the Basic Skills Agency supported local initiatives in family literacy. It encouraged partners, such as primary schools, colleges and community education centres to set up initiatives which enabled:

• parents to improve their own basic skills;

• children to gain support in their literacy and language development;

• parents to discover ways of supporting their children's learning in literacy.

The funding given by the Agency ranged from under £1,000 up to a maximum of £5,000. In each case, the amount granted by the Agency was matched by funding from local sources. Within the broad outline of guidelines set out by the Agency, local partnerships were able to develop patterns of family literacy which were suited to local circumstances and communities. The nature of the small grants programme enabled a larger number of organisations and initiatives to be involved than in the more intensive demonstration programmes which worked to a closely specified model.

In the programme, organisations were invited to bid to the Basic Skills Agency for funding to facilitate local work in family literacy. Different approaches to working with parents with low levels of basic skill in literacy and their children were encouraged. The aim was to improve parents' skills in literacy, support children's literacy and language development, and to extend parents' confidence in helping their children's literacy development.

Family literacy initiatives were to be developed by organisations and agencies working collaboratively.

9

CHAPTER TWO

Description of the range of family literacy small grants programmes

IN 1994, when the research started, approximately 150 small grants initiatives had been funded, and more were still being funded, by the Basic Skills Agency. There was a wide range of programmes throughout England and Wales. Some were in large urban areas, others in suburban areas and small rural towns. We chose 20 programmes in different regions for our study, although two were eventually excluded because of delayed starting dates. Within the original 20, we aimed to include a range of approaches, locations and target populations of parents and children. Although different, all these programmes aimed to establish an inter-generational approach to family literacy.

There are different ways of understanding the term 'inter-generational'. In this study we use it in the sense of including provision to improve the literacy skills of both children and parents. All the family literacy initiatives included in our study aimed to establish the three elements of provision which contributed to this definition of inter-generational.

We will outline some of the key features of the programmes studied and give examples of three different types of provision which were included in our final sample of 18.

Features of the 18 family literacy small grants programmes involved in the research:

- they were located throughout England and Wales, in all kinds of communities and neighbourhoods.

- primary schools had a key role in the local development of family literacy. In most cases, at least a part of the family literacy work was based in a primary school. Only a small number of programmes did not involve schools at all. One of these was based in a social services' family centre; another in an adult education centre and FE college.

- the majority of programmes were based in one location for all aspects of their work. Few programmes were held in more than one place.

- all family literacy sessions took place during the day, usually in school hours; most were held once a week.

- the length of family literacy programmes varied from 10 weeks to 26 weeks.

- the majority of programmes provided a continuous course for a fixed number of weeks, but there were some which offered 'drop in' or individual workshop sessions.

- four programmes were specifically aimed at bilingual parents who had a first language which was not English. One programme had a mixed group of English first-language speakers and bilingual parents.

- new provision was almost always established for family literacy. Only a small number of small grants programmes made use of existing provision or facilities.

- joint sessions for parents and children together were organised in the majority of programmes.

- typically the family literacy programmes were staffed by adult basic skills tutors and primary school teachers.

Each programme is described in detail in Appendix 1.

What did the programmes aim to do?

Many of the programmes had similar aims. The most common ones specified in the proposals for funding were:

- to help parents to support children in their literacy and language development (specified by 17 programmes in the sample);

- to establish inter-generational learning (12 programmes);

- to improve parents' basic skills (11 programmes);

- to improve parents' and children's oral communication skills (9 programmes);

- to raise parents' self-esteem and confidence (9 programmes);

- to improve relations between school and home (9 programmes).

Other aims included the following:

- to help parents gain a qualification (specified by 5 programmes);

- to provide language support for bilingual parents (3 programmes);

- to include community languages in family literacy (2 programmes – these were also included in the 3 programmes offering support for bilingual parents);

- to involve fathers in family literacy (1 programme).

This analysis of programme aims was based on the proposals submitted to the Basic Skills Agency in their application for funding. Although clear aims and outcomes were identified for each programme at the outset, several programmes found that further aims and outcomes were identified as the initiative got underway. Most programmes stated both general and specific aims.

The intended outcomes of family literacy programmes

The intended outcomes which were identified in programmes' proposals also varied. Some were specific and detailed such things as recruitment targets and accreditation levels for parents, or changes in the use made of facilities such as libraries. For example:

- 11 programmes identified accreditation of parents, or volunteers, as an outcome (1 programme even specified percentages of adults to achieve particular levels of accreditation). In 6 of these, Wordpower was the preferred form of accreditation, and in 4 Open College accreditation was chosen. In one example, the form of accreditation was not specified.

- 10 programmes specified the recruitment of a particular target group (8 of these specified the number of participants which they aimed to recruit).

- 7 programmes specified that adults would access other educational or vocational training provision.

- 3 specified increased membership and use of libraries as an intended outcome.

Other intended outcomes were concerned more with the development of effective work in family literacy. For example:

- 11 programmes intended to establish a model for future family literacy work.

- 5 programmes intended to train and (where appropriate) accredit volunteers to work with families.

- 4 programmes stated the production of teaching, learning or information resources as an outcome.

The ways in which aims and intended outcomes were stated reflected differences in mission, professional language and previous experience of local partnerships. It was apparent that some family literacy programmes involved partners who had experience of writing proposals for funding and were aware of the need to specify realistic aims and outcomes. Others, often with less or no previous experience of such development work, presented aims and intended outcomes in more generalised terms.

Examples of the structure and approach of some family literacy small grants programmes

We have indicated the range of provision found across the small grants programmes and their different aims and intended outcomes. In the remaining part of this chapter, we outline three brief examples of approaches to family literacy.

Example 1: A programme which offered a continuous course for parents and children

This programme involved a partnership between an infant school and the local community education federation in an area of high unemployment in Wales. The programme was based in an infant school and was aimed at the parents of selected children in the under-five's class (ages 3-5) of an infant school. It ran as a continuous course on one afternoon a week, for ten weeks. The co-ordinator was a basic skills tutor, based at the community education centre in that area. The tutor was responsible for day-to-day planning, co-ordination and management; and was directly involved in the delivery of adult and joint sessions within the family literacy programme She liaised closely with the infant school's headteacher and the early years teacher who ran the sessions for children.

The content of the programme as a whole, and each individual session, was negotiated and planned jointly by the basic skills tutor and the early years teacher. The content of the sessions for children was planned so that it would enhance and supplement the work done in the rest of the curriculum. The sessions for parents and parents and children together were planned by the basic skills tutor, who matched the content of the session to the requirements of Wordpower at Foundation Level. Wordpower and its assessment was explained to the parents who were given the choice of participating and having their work accredited. The sessions involving parents and children together were taught collaboratively by the early years teacher and the basic skills tutor. The children were taught in a classroom and the adult and joint sessions were usually held in the school library or wet/kitchen area.

The sessions were organised so that they started and ended at the same time as the school afternoon. Children and parents worked on their own for the first hour and, for the second, they undertook joint literacy and language-related activities which were closely related to what had been done in the individual sessions. Follow-up work for parents to try with children at home was usually suggested. To fulfil the requirements for Wordpower accreditation, the adults also had to complete a number of tasks involving reading and writing at home. The family literacy programme was evaluated and a presentation ceremony was held in the school for parents who had completed the course.

Example 2: A programme which was based in a family centre

This example of family literacy involved partnership between a further education college, a local authority Social Services' family centre, and the Rotary Club. The programme was co-ordinated by a basic skills tutor at the college and based at the family centre which served a housing estate on the edge of a cluster of towns in the south-east of England. The programme worked with families which were already clients of the family centre. Parents and children of the ten families involved were invited to participate in family literacy in addition to their overall development programme within the centre. Family literacy took place on one morning a week over the period of one academic year. An experienced basic skills tutor was employed as tutor for the parents and joint sessions. The programme began by concentrating on the parents' own needs in literacy and communication skills and helped to build confidence and to identify ways in which they could support their children's language and literacy development through everyday activities in the home. At a later stage, the programme involved a session where parents and children worked together.

Interesting features of this programme were that it was located in a family centre, set up under the provisions of the 1991 Children's Act, and worked with a closely-targeted client group; and also that child-care facilities were provided whilst the parents worked on their own. Child-care was provided by students at the further education college, on placement, as part of a BTEC nursery nurse course. The placement was supervised by a lecturer in early-childhood education at the college. Transport was provided for families to and from home and the family centre. This allowed parents to take part in family literacy provision with ease.

Example 3: A project which used parents' creative and organisational skills

This example of family literacy provision centred around the planning, construction and use of story-sacks. These were decorated cloth bags which contained a picture story-book and a range of toys and activities designed to encourage and enhance story sharing between parents and children. The story-sack idea originated with the headteacher of a local primary school who involved a group of parents in designing, making and piloting the use of the sacks. The parents were assisted by an early years teacher, an adult basic skills tutor from the local FE college and the headteacher, who managed the whole project. Once underway, the project expanded to include other schools and agencies.

This example of family literacy was interesting because instead of providing a specific course for parents and children to follow, it drew upon their creative and practical abilities as a focus for developing parents' basic skills. The story-sack programme had a clear focus and was based on a simple but very effective idea which motivated both parents and children to participate in book-related activities.

The literacy and communication skills of parents were developed during the course of the story-sack project. In the initial stages, this involved decisions about the appropriate content of the story-sacks. Parents evaluated a range of children's story-books and chose which ones would be most appropriate for the age of the children involved and which would lend themselves to the development of a range of games and activities. From this they drew up criteria and guidelines about the types of book which were most suited to the story-sack concept. The parents' organisational and communication skills were developed in planning the stages of story-sack construction, devising a timetable for work and in allocating tasks to everyone. Once the sacks were made there was discussion, piloting and evaluation of the kinds of activities which could be shared with children using the story-sack materials.

When a large enough number of sacks were made (approximately 100) and they had been successfully used with children, parents were involved in setting up a story-sack lending library system and in running workshops to show how they could be used to promote literacy development at home.

These summaries are intended give a flavour of the different sorts of local provision made within the small grants programme. Details of the different types of content and teaching approaches for the different elements of family literacy found in the 18 programmes are outlined in Chapter 5.

CHAPTER THREE

Outline of the research

———

THE first part of this chapter indicates the aims of the research and the rationale for our approach; the second part gives a short description of how it was conducted.

The Basic Skills Agency had already commissioned the NFER to undertake a detailed evaluation of its four demonstration programmes over a two-year period. These demonstration programmes worked to a very clear and specific model of delivery and organisation which was intensive and involved a relatively high level of funding. The NFER study evaluated the extent to which this model worked in raising the literacy standards of both parents and children (Brooks et al, 1996).

As discussed earlier in Chapter One, the small grants programme was intended to complement the demonstration programmes by· encouraging local, smaller-scale initiatives in family literacy which involved a range of partners. Research on the small grants programme was undertaken by a team from Exeter University. It began in October 1994 and ended in October 1995.

The aim of the research was to look more closely at the approaches to family literacy which were being developed locally rather than to test whether an inter-generational approach to family literacy worked. The intention was:

- to examine which approaches to family literacy were effective;

- to analyse practical lessons for future development in family literacy.

Rationale for our approach

The nature of the small grants programme meant that research needed to be undertaken in a way which was sensitive to local circumstances and contexts. When we started to collect data, some programmes were just beginning, whilst others were already underway. As new applications were still being funded by the Agency, between November, 1994 and May, 1995, some small grants programmes which began during this period were included. Not all programmes had completed their work when the research ended.

Indices of effectiveness

One of the tasks of the research was to identify indices of effectiveness for the work undertaken within the small grants programme. The NFER evaluation of the family literacy demonstration programmes had already provided clear evidence of gains in parents' and children's literacy. The aim of the research on the small grants initiatives was to find a means of comparing diverse forms of local provision.

For sound educational reasons, pre and post programme testing of parents' levels of literacy and other communication skills, using a uniform measure, was rarely conducted. It was important that measures, or indices of progress, were locally-chosen and consistent with the practices of agencies and schools within the small grants scheme. Most family literacy programme tutors preferred informal means of assessing adults, which were usually developed from previous work. Initial diagnostic assessments of parents' basic skills in literacy frequently took place during informal interviews with programme tutors. Children were usually identified by the schools involved, through their normal assessment procedures.

Our aim was to examine the different types of provision in the small grants programme and to indicate which seemed to be most effective and likely to be sustainable in other contexts. For this reason, we examined not only individuals' progress but also factors such as recruitment and retention of suitable parents and children.

The key areas within which programmes could be compared were:

- the ways in which each local family literacy programme established inter-generational work in line with the definition of inter-generational given in Chapter Two.

- the extent to which programmes recruited and retained an appropriate group of parents and children.

- the impact of family literacy on parents, children and home activity; and also on the partner organisations/agencies.

- the extent to which local work in family literacy could be sustained in the longer term.

Forms of data collected and frequency of data collection

Each small grants programme selected for the research was visited several times and different types of information and evidence were collected. These included information on the processes involved in designing and setting up the programmes, including partnership arrangements and strategic planning at area or institutional level. They also included information about the family literacy curriculum, the forms of delivery, staffing and location of programmes.

Quantitative data

For each of the programmes quantifiable information was collected, relating to the location, staffing and partnership arrangements. Where available, data on programme outcomes was also collected. These included details of recruitment and retention of participants, numbers accredited and numbers of parents who progressed to other forms of educational provision, training or employment after participating in family literacy. Where clear evidence was available on parents' and children's progress in literacy during the programme, this was also collected.

Information about individual participants such as age, educational background, number and ages of children and reasons for participating in family literacy was also collected. Profiles of individual parents and their children were constructed.

Qualitative data

Sessions with parents and children were observed, and a range of people involved in each programme was interviewed. We aimed to interview each of the parents at least once; and to interview key staff at the beginning and towards the end of each programme. The people interviewed included:

- the different partners involved in small grants programmes, including those responsible for strategic planning and making policy decisions;

- programme co-ordinators and other administrators;

- adult basic skills tutors;

- teachers and other staff in schools, family centres, community centres;

- parents involved in family literacy programmes;

- children (where possible);

- Basic Skills Agency Development Officers.

Information and documentation relating to various aspects of programme delivery, administration and management were collected. This included, wherever possible:

- examples of planning;

- curriculum organisation;

- teaching material and resources;

- work produced by the participants (parents and children);

- accreditation arrangements and the progression of parents.

Each example of family literacy provision funded within the small grants programme undertook a final evaluation of its own provision, identifying the extent to which its aims were met and improvements to parents' and children's literacy achieved. Where interim and final evaluations were available, they were also included in our analysis.

CHAPTER FOUR

Developing a family literacy curriculum: the range of activities and teaching approaches in small grants programmes

IN this chapter, we examine the different types of family literacy provision developed by the 18 programmes involved in the research. A more detailed picture of the activities and teaching approaches is provided for each element of provision; that is: parents' sessions, children's sessions and the joint sessions.

In Chapter Two, we suggested that there were key areas of similarity and difference in the ways that local provision developed, and one of the most important of these was the extent to which programmes developed inter-generational provision. In some cases, there was clear provision for parents, children and joint work from the very beginning, whereas in other programmes full inter-generational provision was developed more gradually.

Different approaches to inter-generational provision

Outlined below are some examples of how programmes made provision for parents and children and for joint work.

Programmes which developed all three elements of family literacy

Five programmes provided parallel sessions for adults and children, with additional provision for joint adult-child sessions from beginning to end. A common pattern was for family literacy sessions to be held on one morning or afternoon a week during the school day, and to last for 1.5 to 3 hours. There was a period of 1 to 2 hours for adults and children to work separately and a further period of 0.5 to 1 hour for joint adult-child work.

A further two made clear provision throughout for adult sessions and joint adult-child sessions, but less clear provision for children. In both instances, the children involved were within the age range of National Curriculum Key Stage 2. Support was provided for children, but family literacy provision was not clearly differentiated from the normal curriculum, or existing support for learning within the school.

In these two programmes, the joint sessions were held at a different time and did not follow on directly from the sessions for parents and children. One of the two used different venues for the adult and child and joint sessions. This example of family literacy started with joint adult-child sessions in the partner infant school, staffed by a reception class teacher. The children were of pre-school age and were due to start at the school in the following September. There was a rolling programme of six-week sessions for adults and children. These concentrated on basic skills and strategies for supporting children's literacy and language development and, for children, pre-literacy and language development activities. Not all parents who attended the joint sessions at the infant school took up the separate adult-child provision at the community education centre. Family literacy provision in this case was designed to use existing facilities and staffing, for at least part of the programme.

In the other example, parents initially received home tuition on a one-to-one basis with a basic skills tutor, and at a later stage attended a weekly session held in their children's junior school. During this period, the children received in-class support whilst following the normal school curriculum. At a later stage in the programme, joint sessions were undertaken.

Programmes which developed parent and joint sessions

Six programmes made clear, sustained provision for parent and joint sessions. One of these had yet to develop any separate provision for children, whilst two used existing facilities for children within school. The remaining three provided crèche facilities for pre-school children in which there were some literacy and language-related activities.

In two of the above examples, parent and joint sessions ran concurrently. The joint sessions usually followed the sessions for parents. In the other four, the parent and joint sessions were developed at different stages in the programme. One of these was based in a Social Services' Family Centre and started with provision for parents, whilst children were looked after by nursery nurse trainees from the partner Further Education College. An element of joint parent-child work was developed at a later stage.

Five programmes ran regular sessions for parents with some provision for children. Two of these programmes had a workshop or drop-in format, instead of, or in addition to, continuous course provision. For example, in one programme, parents made toys, games and other resources related to particular story-books. The 'story-sacks' thus produced were to be loaned to families to use in shared reading with their children. The parents organised their own work schedule, designed the format, chose stories and other resources for inclusion in the sacks and suggested activities which could be developed from the stories; they also piloted the story-sacks with children.

In another example, a rolling programme of five-week courses in different locations was offered. In these, workshops were provided related to the literacy-learning difficulties of parents and children. They included sessions on how parents could access existing learning support, and the strategies they could use to help their children's literacy and language development. Some of the sessions involved joint work, but there was no clear or consistent provision for joint parent-child sessions.

In the sixth example, parents initially received home tuition on a one-to-one basis with a basic skills tutor, and at a later stage attended a weekly session held in their children's junior school. During this period, the children received in-class support whilst following the normal school curriculum. At a later stage in the programme, joint sessions were undertaken.

The range of activities and teaching approaches

Parent sessions

In the programmes which ran as a continuous course, most of the sessions provided for parents had two related aims:

- the improvement of the parents' basic skills in literacy and communication;

- preparation and support for the literacy and language-related activities in the joint parent-child sessions.

The sessions for parents included activities such as:

- Reading and giving instructions: what makes them clear and easy to understand?

- Comparing and evaluating recipes for making play-dough at home and deciding which one was clearest and easiest to follow.

- Discussion of ways in which activities in the home/family context could promote children's language and literacy: for example, reading and discussion of children's story-books; the language children used; literacy and language activities and games to share with children.

- How watching television with children could be used to promote literacy.

- Evaluation and discussion of television programmes suitable for children.

- Telling and writing stories.

- Parents discussed their own memories of school. Each chose a particular incident to retell.

- Writing about memories of school.

- Choosing books for children.

- Making books with children, making puppets related to children's stories and other book-related activities.

- Examining and evaluating toys and games.

- Discussion about the kinds of games and literacy-related activities which could be made or organised easily and cheaply at home.

- Planning and organising a visit to the local library; reading maps and planning the best route from school to library; writing to library staff; organising other trips, such as a camping expedition.

- Dealing with formal and informal written communication such as complaints, requests, providing information, for example: writing and reading letters to and from children's schools, letters and other forms of written communication relating to everyday life.

Some programmes were not organised as a continuous course. Content in such examples tended to be related to a particular project, such as making resources to support literacy. The story-sack project described briefly earlier was an example of this.

Another example was a programme in a city which worked with a particular ethnic minority community within which there were a large number of refugee families. The sessions for adult participants took the form of English language provision for elder siblings of children in primary school and a series of workshops aimed at the production of traditional oral stories in written form, in both English and the language of the community. These workshop sessions involved the recording, transcription, translation, illustration and printing of traditional, oral stories from the community language into English. The dual-text reading materials were to be introduced and used by the volunteers with younger children in primary school. The second phase of the programme involved parents being invited into school to participate in story-telling and literacy-related activities.

In only two of the programmes visited, was the content of the sessions for parents focused on supporting children's language and literacy development and learning through home activities, rather than clearly emphasising the aim of improving parents' basic skills. However, in a wide range of sessions observed, activities had the dual purpose of providing basic skills support for parents, whilst also showing how they could help their children's literacy learning.

Teaching approaches within the parent/adult sessions

In the main, the sessions for parents and other adults were taught by qualified and experienced adult basic skills tutors, in some cases supported by volunteers. The parents' sessions observed were sensitive to the needs of adult learners and included whole group discussion, group and pair work, and individual tasks. Several programmes used community and family activities and events as a starting point for work with adults. The sessions generally began with an informal whole-group discussion led by the tutor. These discussions included orientation to the content of the session and a review and evaluation of the previous session with comment on work undertaken since then. Tutors encouraged the participation of all parents and encouraged the less confident parents to contribute to discussions; they also kept the discussion focused and related to the planned activity or task.

The parents' sessions usually involved practical activities which were introduced and usually modelled by the tutor, before being undertaken by parents. In almost all the sessions observed, tutors skilfully drew upon adults' own experience as parents, or as learners themselves, as part of the activity or topic. It is easy to undervalue this skill, but it was clearly a contributory factor to the success of many of the parents' sessions.

Tutors offered individual support and guidance where needed and discreetly monitored individual and group progress as the tasks were completed. Although activities were often demanding and challenging, a key element seemed to be the good humour evident in sessions and the trust developed within the group and between the group and the tutor. Frequently, there was time for parents to prepare for the joint sessions with their children, and to 'rehearse' and discuss with each other particular tasks to be done later with the children.

Many parents were apprehensive about returning to learning and were lacking in confidence at the beginning of the programme. A key element in the success of the adult sessions seemed to be the fostering of a positive and cohesive atmosphere within the group, which was supportive yet stimulating, offering encouragement to complete work for accreditation. Because programmes recruited mostly female parents, the focus of sessions tended to be on topics which might be regarded as female-oriented. Clearly, this is a sensitive issue in relation to equal opportunities.

Teaching approaches within programmes aimed at parents whose first language was not English

Four programmes within the sample made provision for parents who were speakers of other languages. Three of these targeted particular ethnic minority communities which had a language or languages in common. One programme recruited a number of parents whose first language was not English, along with those who were mother-tongue English speakers.

At least two of the programmes aimed at bilingual parents recruited volunteers from the community who were fluent in English as well as speaking the dominant community language. In at least one of these, the English as a second language tutor was bilingual and a member of the ethnic minority community. Two of the programmes aimed at bilingual parents offered some home delivery of family literacy.

A particular example was a programme which worked with Muslim women in purdah, who rarely left their homes, other than accompanied by male relatives. The teaching approach adopted was to train volunteer tutors who then worked with the mothers on an individual basis. This seemed to be a particularly successful approach to working with speakers of languages other than English, as it reached a group of parents which had been previously difficult to reach. It also recruited strongly (20 volunteers in all) and had a relatively low drop-out rate – only two people.

Another programme recruited volunteer tutors, in this case bilingual young people who were unemployed. These volunteers were offered English language support and worked within the community to raise awareness of the importance of the family's role in promoting literacy. They also spent time in primary schools working with younger siblings. An interesting feature of this programme was that it not only offered support for the development of literacy in English, but also made links between the predominantly oral cultural traditions of story-telling within the community language and literacy in English. A further feature of this programme was its wider understanding of family. A programme tutor explained to the researcher that in this particular community, the concept of family was more than just parents and children. In recruiting young people who were elder siblings and cousins to make links between parents and the younger children's schools, this programme offered an approach to family literacy provision which was sensitive to local cultural and social needs.

Content of joint parent/child sessions

Joint sessions for parents and children emphasised the process of sharing activities involving literacy and language. Joint sessions were almost always preceded by preparatory work in the separate adult or child sessions. Interviews with adult participants confirmed that they were keen to learn and develop ways of supporting their children and sharing activities and experiences. Activities in the joint sessions included:

- sharing stories and books together;

- making play-dough – with parents and children following recipes and measuring and weighing ingredients;

- visiting a library;

- making an alphabet scrap-book;

- constructing alphabets;

- sorting games whilst shopping;

- describing and guessing objects in a 'feely bag';

- making cards at Easter and Christmas and for special occasions;

- making glove puppets and devising stories and games with these;

- writing poems together.

Both tutors and parents reported that the Basic Skills Agency's *Read and Write Together* packs were useful in presenting ideas for joint reading and writing activities.

The joint sessions were most usually staffed by a combination of both adult basic skills tutors and teachers or other staff. In some (but not all) programmes offering joint sessions, the planning was undertaken collaboratively by the tutors involved. In a number of programmes the planning was largely the responsibility of one tutor, supported by the other. Parents were encouraged to take the lead in activities with children. In most of the joint sessions observed, the tutors responsible supported parents and offered unobtrusive support and teaching, often through making suggestions or asking questions.

The connection between the joint and separate sessions was particularly important for the adult participants. The preparatory work and discussions in the separate parents' or adults' sessions modelled and prepared for the activities with children. Several parents said that they found the preparation done earlier gave them the confidence to focus on the language and literacy dimensions of joint activities which they might not otherwise have done.

Some parents told us that before they joined the family literacy group, they believed that school was where children learned and that they saw home activities as being unrelated to learning. One of the clearest messages to come from parents was the way in which the family literacy sessions, particularly the joint sessions with children, had validated the importance of what could be done at home which supported children's learning.

Activities and teaching in sessions for children

Fewer programmes developed a consistent programme of separate sessions for children. Only five held regular separate sessions for children, and a further two programmes made some provision for children. Those which achieved consistent separate provision for children all worked with the pre-school or reception age-group. Sessions for children were usually led by an early years specialist, often a teacher, but in one case by a pre-school play-group leader working with the family literacy programme. The activities generally involved the children in practical tasks related to language development, pre-and early literacy activities and the provision of opportunities for literacy-related play. Important areas of work with children included:

- awareness of the alphabet and letters, for example letters of children's own names and those of their families;

- the development of phonological awareness i.e. sound patterns and repetition, play with sound and words;

- sound/ letter correspondence;

- emphasis on the development of hand-eye co-ordination and fine motor skills, such as handling pencils and pens, scissors, gluing objects, using building blocks.

Individual sessions which we observed included:

- alphabet games;

- nursery rhymes, songs and clapping games;

- story-telling and reading, activities related to books, for example puppet shows;

- practical or construction tasks with a language component, such as weighing, sorting and making comparisons between things;

- dramatic play, including a play library and post-office;

- making greeting cards; painting and collage making;

- drawing and writing, including the use of writing areas with pens and pencils, computers and different types of paper and card;

- collaborative poetry writing.

Teaching approaches in the children's sessions combined whole group work, small group and individual work.

Typically, the children might be gathered together at the beginning of a session with the teacher or session leader for discussion, story-reading or telling. Then there might be a demonstration of an activity by the session leader, followed by the children undertaking a practical activity themselves; sometimes alone, sometimes working with other children. During the course of a session, there would usually be a range of different activities for children, to provide variety and to maintain children's interest and attention. Whilst children were doing practical activities, teachers and session leaders offered support, encouragement and help to children, and where appropriate asked questions to lead them further in the task. An example of an effective session for children is outlined later in this chapter.

Provision for older children

The two programmes which included an element of provision for older school-age children had a considerable task in designing and delivering an appropriate curriculum. In these cases, particularly where children were at Key Stage 2 of the National Curriculum, the purpose of the provision within family literacy was to enable children to recover any lack of progress in the development of literacy or communication and, ultimately, to progress to an acceptable level of achievement within their normal class.

In one school, a coherent and successful system of learning recovery and support already existed, staffed by a special needs teacher. The family literacy programme made use of this provision for children, although those whose parents had basic skills needs were not distinguished from others within the organisation of the sessions. The provision for children was consistent, appropriately staffed and explicitly integrated into the school's larger aims and curriculum requirements, (as evidenced in the school's OFSTED inspection report), but it did not quite meet the requirement of family literacy programmes to make separate provision for those children whose parents had low basic skills in literacy. In this case, where the school had good quality existing provision in learning support, separate additional child-only sessions within the school would not necessarily have been helpful. Furthermore, the programme budget was not large enough to provide the teacher's salary for separate sessions for these children, each week. Even had the budget allowed for this staffing, school and programme staff questioned whether a teacher of the same calibre as the special needs post-holder would be found for a small number of hours per week.

Why was developing effective separate work with children a challenge to so many programmes?

We have indicated above that whilst all programmes developed work with parents, and most developed effective joint parent child sessions, effective separate work with children presented a greater challenge. There were several reasons for this, some of which have been indicated already. Overall factors constraining the development of consistent and effective work with children included:

- concerns about disrupting children's normal school routine; particularly that they would miss some mainstream curriculum provision if involved in family literacy;

- reluctance on the part of early years teachers in schools to dedicate time to a small group of children, rather than teaching the whole class;

- lack of financial resources to pay for an adult basic skills tutor and an early years teacher;

- shortage of space to accommodate separate provision for children which paralleled the parent sessions.

It is important to emphasise that schools were highly supportive of family literacy and often made considerable efforts to offer practical assistance in keeping a programme going. However, an issue which needed further clarification was the specific nature of the benefits which children of school age might gain from being involved in family literacy.

An example of a programme which achieved effective inter-generational provision, with sessions for parents, children and joint work

In one programme, effective sessions for both children and parents and a joint session were observed. We chose to describe this session because not only were each of the separate strands effective, but the overall coherence and co-ordination of each element was also excellent.

The sessions were held in an infant school. Work with parents was held in a welcoming and comfortably furnished library and resources area and was led by an experienced basic skills tutor. The children's session was held in a classroom with appropriate resources and provision for play activities, and was led by an early years teacher in the school. The afternoon's work had been planned jointly by the basic skills tutor and the early years teacher. The content of each element had been matched carefully to ensure coherence between each strand and to maximise the likely success of the joint parent-child session.

The parents' session

The focus for the parents' sessions was on reading, evaluating and following instructions. The adult basic skills tutor introduced the afternoon's session by indicating what the group would be doing that afternoon with their children – making play-dough. She then moved on to discuss, with the whole group, the best ways of organising an activity with children in the kitchen. She skilfully introduced the notion of having clear instructions to follow to help in the task. Continuing discussion with the whole group, the tutor asked them to consider whether all written instructions were clear to a reader. The group indicated very strongly that this was not always the case and that some instructions were extremely complicated and difficult to follow.

They then considered criteria for making instructions clear. Following this group discussion, the tutor introduced three versions of a recipe for making children's play-dough at home. She divided the parents into pairs or groups of three and asked them to evaluate the examples given and to identify which they preferred and why. After time to work on this task, the parents reconvened as a whole group and compared their evaluations. After much discussion agreement was reached on which was the best version of the recipe. At this stage the tutor began to prepare the parents for working with the children and to consider how they would assist the children in making play-dough by following the instructions. They were asked to predict how their children would approach the task and what problems they might experience in working together. There was also a general discussion of how such an activity would help to develop children's language and literacy-awareness.

The children's session

The children's session was led by the early years teacher and complemented the parents' work. It also prepared children for the joint session which was to follow, in the second part of the afternoon. The work involved sorting objects into sets: identifying what belonged in one group and why other things did not belong in that group. The teacher also led the children towards comparing objects and substances, and describing differences and similarities between them. For example, was one object bigger than another? Was there more liquid in one container than another, and how could they tell? She also provided some of the substances which would be used in the play-dough activity and asked the children about these. Was there more flour than water? Was the flour heavier than the water? The children also described the texture and consistency of substances and mixtures.

Towards the end of the session the teacher talked with the children about helping to make things in the kitchen. Did they ever help to make things; and what? How did their mothers and fathers go about making things? Here she introduced the idea of following instructions and recipes, and how we could read a recipe which would tell us how to do something and what we would need to have to follow it. The session ended by the children being told that after a break they would be working with their parents, making play-dough. There was a high level of engagement and enthusiasm throughout the session and great excitement at the prospect of the joint activity!

The joint session

For the second part of the afternoon, parents and children worked together, guided by both the basic skills tutor and the early years teacher. The session was held in the classroom in which the children had worked earlier. The room contained both a sink and a cooker. Between them, the two staff had brought in all the equipment and provisions which would be needed to make the play-dough. Each parent worked with her child, explaining what they were going to do and how. The parents involved the children in the activity and encouraged them to describe the ingredients used and what they were doing – for example stirring the mixture slowly, to predict what they would need to do next. Each of the parents used the recipe and consulted it when needed. They talked to the children about following the recipe, saying such things as ' Let me check what comes next. What does the recipe say?' Once the play-dough had been made, parents encouraged their children to play with it, rolling it out and making it into shapes with pastry cutters. At the end of the afternoon, the children took the play-dough home with them.

Both parts of the afternoon were highly enjoyable for both parents and children. An additional feature of the sessions was that the parents' separate work and that done with their children was matched to the requirements of Wordpower Foundation Level accreditation.

What made this a successful example of inter-generational work?

• Provision of coherent and interesting separate sessions for parents and children, leading to appropriate joint work.

• Close match of content between the parents' and children's session. Each strand was interesting and appropriate in its own right and complemented the other strands.

- Clear planning and co-ordination for the parents' and children's sessions.

- Co-operation and team-work between the adult basic skills tutor and the early years teacher.

- An appropriate location, setting and timing for the sessions.

In this chapter we have indicated the extent to which programmes achieved inter-generational provision and the forms which this took. It is clear that many programmes experienced a substantial challenge in achieving all three strands of family literacy provision. In particular good quality, sustained provision for children of school-age seemed to be problematic for small grants programmes to achieve. However, we have given a detailed example from one programme which did achieve good quality provision in all three elements of family literacy, and we have indicated reasons why this programme was successful.

CHAPTER FIVE

Recruiting families

‾‾‾‾‾‾

THIS chapter examines the methods used to recruit suitable families. One of the key aims of family literacy programmes was to reach parents with low levels of basic skill in literacy. Thus the recruitment of appropriate participants was fundamental to the success of small grants programmes. However, the practicalities of recruiting parents with low levels of literacy, who had young children of pre-school or school age, was a substantial challenge for most, if not all, programmes.

The approaches used to identify and recruit families

Programmes obviously used a variety of methods to recruit participants. They are summarised below:

- The most common way of reaching parents was by personal contact: 9 programmes reached parents through word-of mouth or personal contact.

- The next most popular method was the use of printed advertisements, letters and circulars. This approach was used by 7 programmes.

- Only one programme recruited parents and their children through a partner agency's referral system – although participation in family literacy was on a voluntary basis.

- One programme used a range of approaches for different strands of the provision. These included letters to parents of children about to start school, inviting them to attend; sensitive personal contact with selected families in a particular community; flyers and leaflets advertising the 'Getting into Books' programme. Approximately 40% of those contacted later attended the joint sessions.

Although the figures above provide an over-view of the range and popularity of methods of recruitment, practice across programmes was more complex. Some programmes tried different approaches at different times in the recruitment process. Personal contact with potential recruits took a variety of forms. For example, teachers in children's schools approached individual parents informally at the beginning or end of the school day and suggested that they might like to come to the family literacy sessions. In at least two cases, recruitment was done initially by an informal invitation at a parents' evening. In one area family literacy aimed to reach the women in a Muslim ethnic minority community. Volunteer tutors who were part of, or had access to, the informal family and social networks were used to identify and approach women who might benefit from involvement in family literacy, and later to help provide home tuition.

It was clear that personal contact with parents was a successful way of recruiting. However, there was no single means of making this contact. What worked depended a great deal on:

- the community in which the family literacy programme was situated and the social networks within it;

- the relationship between schools and parents;

- the degree of familiarity and previous experience programme staff, particularly basic skills tutors, had with the targeted parents.

Successful ways of making contact with parents included:

- teachers talking informally with parents at the beginning and end of the school day;

- programmes holding open days, coffee mornings and other social activities in schools and community centres to introduce family literacy;

- mediation of key community figures such as health visitors, playgroup organisers;

- as programmes developed, parents who had taken part were often valuable in recruiting new participants.

The resourcefulness developed by programme staff in reaching and recruiting parents is well illustrated by the comment from the headteacher of a partner primary school:

> 'We worked out a way of getting through to parents without writing a letter saying, "If you can't read this, come and see me!". What we did was . . . we made a list of the families we knew . . . and we got seven people interested that way . . . I approached one or two people in the playground. The first one I approached said, "Definitely not. No way!" But others were quite grateful. And we started off with our core group . . . but as time is passing through the year we've been able to approach other people – for instance, when a child is on the admissions list and we know the family, or they have admitted having trouble with reading and don't want to fill this form in, then we've been able to say, "Well, don't worry. We've got this group which might help you and your child". One lady was so unsure of herself, she said, "Can I come? I'm pregnant?" I replied, "Of course you can! And bring your baby afterwards"'

(Headteacher, First School)

The most important issues in recruiting parents and children were:

- Maximising existing knowledge, resources and expertise in order to identify and approach parents effectively;
- Careful analysis of the needs of communities and parents to be served by family literacy.

Small grants programmes had differing levels of previous experience and expertise in recruiting the particular groups of people for whom local family literacy programmes were designed. Some programmes involved agencies or individuals with substantial previous experience in recruiting similar groups of people. Some had experience of recruiting for outreach initiatives in adult education which complemented family literacy. Other partners, such as schools, were relatively new to this work, although many had experience of parental involvement schemes.

Previous experience in recruiting similar groups of adults for basic skills courses, or other related work, helped programme staff to identify the best ways of publicising family literacy. In some instances, it helped staff to choose the most appropriate location and time for sessions. Developing and sharing expertise in appropriate recruitment strategies was one aspect in which inter-agency collaboration was particularly important.

Even those programmes with substantial experience of recruiting adults for purposes relevant to family literacy had to adapt to new circumstances. For example, partners with successful experience of recruiting parents for school parental involvement schemes had to learn how to encourage parents with poor basic skills to return to learning . It did not always follow that parents keen to participate in schemes to help their children had poor basic skills, or that those who had poor basic skills would automatically identify family literacy as being appropriate to their needs. Programme staff had to maintain a delicate balance between ensuring that courses and workshops were well-subscribed, and ensuring that the parents who did participate were those who would themselves benefit from family literacy.

It is important to bear in mind that programmes which started with little previous experience gained appropriate knowledge of how to recruit suitable parents for family literacy, during the course of the small grants period. It is likely that such programmes became much more successful in later stages of programme development.

Underlying all the examples of successful recruitment was careful needs analysis in the communities which family literacy was aiming to serve. Programmes which recruited successfully spent a considerable amount of time and effort identifying and making contact with potential participants, before the programme began. In some cases, this was done prior to publicising family literacy.

Family literacy programmes which started with little detailed knowledge of or contact with specific parents in the community were at a disadvantage, and, in general, found recruitment more of a challenge. Such programmes often started with a strong belief that family literacy would be appropriate in a particular community on the basis of indicators of economic disadvantage, for example high take-up of free school meals or high levels of unemployment. These programmes tended to operate an approach to recruitment which might be summarised as *'We know there are parents in need of family literacy out there, but how do we reach them and get them to take part?'*

The match between need, as perceived by programme organisers, and parents' actual desire to participate, was critical to success in recruiting and retaining a cohort of participants. One programme provider emphasised that need could be identified relatively easily. However, in order to be motivated enough to become involved and to complete the programme, participants had to see that family literacy was useful to them and their children:

> *'It's also important to assess 'wants', as opposed to 'needs'. The need is there, but unless people actively desire to do something about it they won't come in. What you seem to identify, is that the people who really need it are not easy to access. Even if you say we'll involve (different agencies) it's not necessarily the case that we'll reach all those people. Also, I suppose different agencies define need in different ways.'*
>
> (Programme provider)

How was family literacy presented to parents?

Programme staff gave careful thought to the messages conveyed in publicity materials and in informal descriptions of family literacy. They wanted to make clear that it offered an opportunity for parents to improve literacy skills and made substantial efforts to avoid stigmatising those with poor basic skills. Below is a summary of the ways in which family literacy was presented to parents.

- 13 programmes gave a clear message that family literacy was intended to help both parents and children.

- 4 gave a stronger message that their aim was primarily to help children.

- 1 programme indicated that its purpose was to address a specific learning difficulty in a family literacy context.

41

Within these three broad categories, there were differences in the extent to which the purposes of family literacy were spelled out to parents. Some made straightforward statements that the purpose of family literacy was to support children in literacy, help parents with their own basic skills, offering the opportunity for external accreditation, and help parents to help their children with language development and literacy. Other programmes suggested that their purpose was to help children settle into school, or for parents to learn how to support their children's school work.

Programmes obviously wished to make family literacy provision attractive to parents and to avoid any potential embarrassment which might be caused by implying that participants had to have low levels of literacy in order to join a family literacy programme. For example, some had titles such as *'Parents and Children Reading Together'*, *'Getting into Books'*, *'Phases and Folio – Information Technology'* or *'Family Learning Through Information Technology'*.

It did not appear to make a difference whether or not programmes used the specific title family literacy in their publicity material, or whether another name was used. What was important in successful recruitment of appropriate parents was that at some stage in the recruitment process the aims of family literacy and its three dimensions were made clear to parents. It was apparent that programmes which had been clear about this aspect of family literacy provision avoided misunderstandings at a later stage in the programme. However, there was no easy solution to the challenge of recruiting parents with poor basic skills – those termed the 'hard to reach' by one programme tutor. This is an area where small grants programmes might be encouraged to share expertise and insights with each other.

Numbers recruited

Outline of participants recruited

- A total of 163 parents participated
- 12 fathers participated

- parents' ages ranged from 17 to 48. Most were in their 20s and 30s

- 49% were between 21 and 30

- 45% were between 31 and 40

- 1.7% were between 17 and 20

- 4.3% were between 41 and 50

- 82% of parents had qualifications which were GCSE grade D or below (or equivalent)

- 47% had left school without formal qualifications

- 18% had qualifications which were GCSE grade C or above

- 25% had a first language other than English

- 11% were single parents

- 346 children took part, 82 were under 5.

The reasons parents gave for joining family literacy programmes

- 55% of parents said they joined a family literacy programme to help their children.

- 26% said they joined to help themselves and/or to help other parents.

- 17% said they joined primarily to help themselves and their children equally.

A high correlation was observed between the messages programmes gave parents and the main reason parents gave for joining (r=0.68). The correlation suggests that publicity materials and recruitment strategies were attracting parents whom they had targeted and were, therefore, generally effective.

Many parents whose initial motivation was to help their child said that they had not thought of learning for themselves until the opportunity had been presented to them. Some also said that they had given up hope of achieving educational success themselves, but were keen to help their children. A large number of parents were able to read and write, but were seeking to be able to write, spell and communicate better. Of the parents who said their prime purpose in joining was to improve their own basic skills as well as to help their children, a very small minority were seeking employment, but most were simply seeking an interest outside their home.

Some of the parents interviewed who were not English first-language speakers, indicated that their desire to learn was linked to being able to communicate effectively in English in their community. For example, in coping with the health problems which affected families, parents – particularly mothers – told of the considerable frustration they had experienced in being unable to communicate directly with doctors and other health professionals. Although some women said they had been helped in the past by members of their extended family, particularly male relatives, all were keen to take advantage of the opportunity to learn once it had been made available to them. However, they also admitted that had the opportunity to become more involved in their child's education not been presented to them directly through a family literacy programme, they would probably not have sought it out for themselves.

Most of the parents recruited were women, regardless of their ethnic origin. As very few of them were in full-time, or even substantial part-time employment, it is reasonable to infer that they were largely occupied with child-care. Many parents told us that it was unlikely that they would have participated in existing educational provision, including basic skills. The reasons they gave were that existing provision tended to be located at a distance from their homes and would not fit in with their family commitments such as taking children to school in the morning, collecting them at lunch-time and in the afternoon. A number of the female parents interviewed said they saw family literacy as a means by which they could be helped to feel better about themselves and to do their best to help their children. Most of the male parents who participated did so with a partner. When interviewed fathers said that they were interested in using what they learned in family literacy to improve their relationship with their children.

Examples of successful approaches to recruiting suitable families

Example A: recruiting hard to reach parents

In the first phase of programme development, a co-ordinator realised that the parents who were already participating in family literacy could have a key role in identifying and encouraging other parents in the community. It was often suggested by parents themselves, who said such things as 'I have this friend who might be interested, but she's a bit worried about coming on her own . . .' or 'I know someone who'd like to come, but she's afraid she'll be much worse than everyone else with her reading and writing . . .'. The programme co-ordinator encouraged parents to bring new recruits, and towards the end of the first phase of family literacy identified existing participants who would be particularly useful in encouraging other parents with less confidence in coming forward, or with poorer basic skills. In this particular case, through skilful negotiation, a programme co-ordinator encouraged a parent who had poor basic skills in to such a networking role and in doing so increased the woman's confidence and ensured her regular commitment to the programme.

Example B: successful identification of an appropriate group of parents for family literacy

In two cases, the basic skills tutor responsible for establishing the family literacy programme had previously established and tutored a parent group within the same two schools as part of the work of the local community education centre. The community education service had been developing work with schools for four years before the start of the family literacy programme. Many of the parents recruited had expressed a desire to support their children's learning, to improve their own basic skills and to undertake further education and training if it fitted with their domestic responsibilities and circumstances. Thus the principle of parents attending their children's school for their own educational purposes, as well as to help their children, had already been established and connections with an appropriate target group developed.

Example C: effective use of staff with knowledge of a particular community

In another programme, which worked with a specific ethnic minority community in a large city, the programme co-ordinator and tutor had undertaken previous work with the target community and had established strong links within it. The programme tutor was qualified and experienced in teaching English to speakers of other languages, and was a member of the ethnic minority community. This gave that person a familiarity with and access to families that other tutors would not have had. Because of such effective staffing for the programme, it was relatively straightforward to identify those who had a need for family literacy. However, ensuring participation of families in all aspects of the programme over a period of time presented a greater challenge.

Example D: using the referral system of a partner agency to identify and contact suitable families

A further example was where the client group for family literacy was identified through referral from a partner agency which had undertaken the needs analysis as part of its own work. Parents identified as likely to benefit from involvement in a family literacy programme were already attending a family centre and were offered the provision as an additional activity. Referral from agencies such as Social Services was a useful way of pooling resources and avoiding the replication of services. However, it was also important that client need, as perceived by the referral agency, was supported by the client's wish to participate in family literacy.

Throughout the family literacy small grants initiative as a whole, there was success in meeting the challenge of identifying and recruiting an appropriate number of suitable parents. Individual small grants programmes achieved different levels of success in the number of parents recruited, although the majority were effective in recruiting enough to sustain the programme. In the initial stages of programme development, there was a clear difference in the level of success experienced by programmes which started with little previous work with the target client group compared with those with more experience. Equally, there was a difference in the level of success experienced by those programmes which deliberately targeted 'hard to reach' parents whose basic skills needs were acute, but who were reluctant to participate in educational activities, or even groups.

Programmes offering some home-based provision did not have the resources to reach the numbers which could be recruited in a group. One effective way of providing home-based delivery was through the sensitive recruitment and training of volunteers within the community targeted. A successful example of this was undertaken working with women in a Muslim ethnic minority community.

There was evidence to suggest that 'hard to reach parents', with very poor basic skills and social confidence, could be reached more effectively at a later stage in programme development. A particularly effective way of encouraging them to come forward was through personal contact with parents who had been successfully involved in family literacy.

Overall, recruitment of the right number of suitable parents with children of a reasonably uniform age was not an easy task. It was a challenge to which programmes rose with impressive vigour. Those programmes which achieved the aim of recruiting an adequate number of appropriate parents to sustain the programme were the ones which undertook rigorous needs analysis in the communities they aimed to serve. Identifying people who wanted to join in family literacy provision was critical to their success.

Less successful were those programmes which identified a need in the abstract, through indicators such as unemployment or high take up of free school meals or a school's identification of children with problems in literacy development. It did not necessarily follow that because an area was economically deprived, family literacy programmes would be well-subscribed.

A further factor in successful recruitment was the effective use of experience gained in previous development work which complemented family literacy. This was one area in which the partnership aspect of the small grants scheme was particularly useful: different partners sometimes had useful expertise or familiarity with a particular group of people.

It was clear that approaching potential recruits through informal personal contact was an effective way to reach suitable parents. Schools had a key role to play in this respect. Conversations with parents when they brought or collected children to and from school were one way of making contact. 'Taster sessions' or open days, such as coffee mornings or demonstrations of aspects of family literacy, were also effective ways of attracting parents. Printed materials such as posters or flyers advertising family literacy were most effectively used as a back up for personal contact. Less effective ways of recruiting suitable parents were through sending letters or publicity materials 'cold' to homes. The parents attracted by such publicity tended to be those who were already able to support their children and had little need of help with their own basic skills.

CHAPTER SIX

What did the family literacy small grants programmes achieve?

THIS chapter indicates the achievements of the small grants programmes in relation to the indices of effectiveness identified in Chapter Three. We outline achievement in relation to the retention of parents; attendance during programmes, rates of accreditation; the progression of parents into other educational provision, training and employment.

Retention and attendance of parents

Once programmes had recruited participants, they tended to retain them. Retention rates across all the programmes studied were generally high. According to the data available from each of the 18 programmes, 41 parents dropped out before the end of the programme – an average of approximately 25%. About half of those who dropped out, or who attended irregularly, gave reasons such as family illness or death, domestic problems, finding employment or moving from the area. A much smaller number said their reasons for dropping out were related to programme factors or group dynamics within the programme. Among this group, reasons given were that the programme did not match their needs, or they felt that they did not fit into the group.

However, some programmes were more successful than others in retaining participants. One programme recruited 20 volunteer tutors to work on an individual out-reach basis with women in an ethnic minority community. In this programme there was a particularly low rate of drop out. Another programme recruited 15 participants and only 4 dropped out. Reasons for high levels of retention were not always related to programme factors. For example in one programme which recruited 8 suitable parents, two dropped out: one because of the death of a close family member and another because she got a job. The parent who dropped out because of family bereavement indicated that she would like to continue in the programme at a later date. Of the remaining parents in this programme, all were committed to the programme, attended regularly and completed Wordpower accreditation.

In another programme, which aimed to reach parents with very low levels of basic skill in literacy, and where the initial stage of the programme was delivered by means of home tuition, only a small number of parents were recruited. However, only one parent dropped out because he felt that he did not need the basic skills support provided. He added that finding this out had helped to raise his confidence. The remaining participants attended regularly throughout the rest of the programme, which lasted for a full school year.

In making any comparative judgement about programmes' success on the basis of retention of parents, it is important to distinguish between programmes which recruited socially and economically vulnerable parents particularly in need of family literacy provision, and those which recruited a wider social range of parents. A programme which was based in a Social Services' family centre served a small number of parents whose domestic circumstances were unstable. Highly stressful family problems, often of considerable severity, were the cause of poor or sporadic attendance. In this particular programme some parents ceased to attend for a considerable period of time, but returned as soon as they were able. Other programmes had a fluctuating population of attendees – some dropped out but were replaced by others who wanted to join the programme after the initial start date.

There did not seem to be any obvious connection between retention and the length or structure of programmes.

Attendance

Calculating the attendance rates of individual adult participants was complex. As already indicated, some programmes lost participants but gained others throughout the programme's duration. Other programmes did not operate as a course, but were a series of workshops, or a group making resources. In these instances it was not appropriate for programme providers to mark attendance. One programme had three different but inter-related strands and not all parents and children attended the separate adult and child sessions.

The length of programmes varied from 10 to 26 weeks. In some cases starting and finishing dates were not easily identifiable as programmes had delayed or staggered starting dates and some even stretched beyond their planned finishing date as more funding became available. Furthermore, some programmes, which organised their adult and joint adult-child sessions on different days, met more than once a week.

All this meant that the use of a single measure – percentage attendance rates – would be a relatively crude measure. Therefore, we calculated only the attendance of those adult parents who had participated in the full programme. It was further decided to treat programmes with more than one cohort as one cohort by amalgamating their data. This led to a third decision, that is, to calculate attendance by individual adult participant rather than by programme attended.

Attendance rates

- 70% of participants had good attendance, i.e. they attended more than 75% of the time;

- 16% had average attendance, i.e., they attended between 50% and 74% of the time;

- 14.5% of participants were classed as having poor attendance rates, i.e. where their attendance was less than 50%.

Parents' and children's progress and other benefits gained from participating in family literacy

Some programmes undertook pre and post programme analysis of participants' competence in literacy, but these were rarely standardised tests. Diagnostic interviews were more commonly used to assess the suitability of adult participants for involvement in family literacy and their specific literacy needs. Where programmes had ended during the course of our study, information on participants' progress was not easily quantifiable: data tended to be in the form of tutor assessments of course-work, student evaluation of the course and self-evaluation reports.

Other indicators of benefits gained and outcomes were in the accreditation and progression rates for programmes. However, at the time when fieldwork was completed, the evidence available to us did not reflect eventual accreditation rates within programmes. Similarly, information on progression rates for adults from family literacy to further education, vocational training or employment was partial. Actual progression into mainstream, full-time further education courses would not be known until students registered for courses, usually in the following academic year. That notwithstanding, there was evidence relating to enrolment into part-time and short courses of further education.

In one programme, for example, children's performance in reading tests was compared before and after the programme. The gains made by children whose parents were in the family literacy programme were almost all greater than those of children whose parents did not attend.

In general, the programmes which had developed provision for children and joint parent-child work, saw the benefits for children as longer term rather than in short term measures of particular skills or competence.

A key benefit for children, aimed for by a number of programmes involving schools, was increased motivation and orientation towards literacy in school. For younger children in family literacy programmes, benefits derived would be qualitative rather than quantitative, marked in ways such as increased awareness of and interest in literacy related activities, or better communicative abilities. Similarly, changes in home practices were reported to the research team, rather than being directly observed. Observation would have required intensive study of families in their homes over a longer period of time.

We were aware of the limitations of self-report, particularly when informants are asked directly whether there has been any change in home practice as a result of involvement in family literacy. Consequently, we used examples of reported home change only when they were volunteered by parents or children during interview or observation, or where they were recorded in writing by parents themselves, for example in home diaries.

The evidence that we were able to gather on benefits to participants and programme outcomes in relation to progression is thus limited both by the nature of the small grants programmes and by the relationship of the research to the programmes. Thus whilst we are not able to quantify such benefits, we are able to give an indication of benefits felt by parents and those indicated by programme staff.

A range of benefits was identified. The main ones, identified in most programmes were:

- parents interviewed in at least 13 programmes indicated an increased understanding of the ways in which they could support their children in literacy and language development and a better understanding of the relationship between home and school in children's education;

- examples of positive change in home practices to provide more opportunities for adult/child interactions and shared literacy events were identified by parents interviewed in at least 10 programmes;

- accreditation for adult learning and, in some cases, progression into further education, vocational training or employment was identified specifically by parents or programme staff in at least 10 programmes;

- greater understanding by adult and early childhood educators of the potential for working with other agencies and phases of education was indicated in at least 15 programmes.

What parents said about the impact of family literacy on home activity and their awareness of their children's literacy development

In at least 10 programmes, where interviewed, parents reported positive changes in children's attitudes to reading and writing, at all ages, as exemplified below. These parents were in most, but not all, cases participating in programmes where there was clear provision for joint work. A notable exception was in a programme where joint parent-child work had not yet begun, but a parent described how her children had seen her reading and writing at home as part of the work for the programme, and how they had begun to read and write with her.

'They (children) want to do writing now . . . they see that I've got my homework and they want to do some too . . .'
(Parent)

At a later stage in the programme, this parent was filmed sharing a book with her children and talking about this.

Not only the parent above, but also others reported that they were more aware of their children's literacy development and felt more confident in being able to offer support and monitor how children were progressing in their reading and writing. In one example, parents watched a video and then discussed children's early development in literacy. This was followed by a joint session in which parents shared the reading of a book with their child and programme staff encouraged parents to watch their children's behaviour with books and other reading materials and to undertake shared reading. A parent later made the following comment about her daughter:

'I have seen a big change in her reaction to books. She really enjoys them now – will sit with them up the right way – pretend to read – follow the picture. Her drawing and writing is starting to follow a good form. Her colouring is getting less hectic'.
(Parent)

Parents in two other programmes indicated how activities involving observation of children and keeping a record of what they did had influenced what they did with their children in the home:

'Because we're making a record of what our children can do and we are paying more attention to it. It makes you more conscious. When they do something new you really think about it and it encourages you to do more with them. Like when he said a few words it encouraged me to speak to him more and bring him out.'
(Parent)

'Well one week we did something whereby we had to write down all the material we read in 24 hours. It really brought me more aware of reading and how important it is. He (her son) benefited from that as well because you had to think about what you were really doing during the day. (Before the course) I wouldn't have thought of sitting down at home and drawing with him or painting with him or something like that. Well I would have thought of it but I wouldn't have made the effort. Now I make more of an effort.'
(Parent)

Another noticed her child's willingness to read voluntarily:

'I couldn't believe it when he brought this pile of books home. I couldn't believe that it was him reading'.
(Parent)

'I tell you what I do now, I don't fob them off. You know when they bring you a picture or something and you say 'oh yes lovely, go and play.' Now I think well he's worked hard on that, he wants me to look at it, which again is all down to this.'
(Parent)

Greater understanding of how children learn literacy, led, in some cases, to parents having more patience with and tolerance of their children's errors in reading and the confidence to help them with difficulties:

'Since I've been coming here I've got more patience with Mark with his reading. He used to come home with a book. He used to read the book and have words on one page and read them and he had the same words on another page and he didn't know them. I used to say well "Mark, you've just said the word" and now he'd say "but I don't know it." I said "but you know you've just said those words'.
(Parent)

'(I've got more) . . . patience, a different outlook on the way the children read and write. My daughter, when she came over in September she was (reading age score) 5 years and 9 months now she's 7 years and 9 months.'

(Parent)

Parents in a programme which set up a lending library to coincide with the course commented on how much they appreciated having a wide range of books available for their children to choose and take home. They also said that they as parents had benefited from seeing different types of books.

Although schools are now more accessible to parents than in the past, many adults still saw a clear distinction between home and school; and their responsibility and that of the school:

'It's not that you don't want to do things to help them, it's knowing what to do to help them, finding the right things to do with them. That's the important thing, that you know that what you're doing, you're doing it to help them.'

(Parent)

'I think you take it for granted. You bring your children up to the age to go to school and then once they go to school you think school is school and home is home.'

(Parent)

There was also evidence of an awareness of inter-generational influences on perceptions and attitudes to school and literacy learning. For example, when adults were asked what their own parents did at home, one responded as follows:

'My mum thinks the old fashioned way – you should take your kids to school and leave them at school. Yes. They're like the old generation. They never came to school unless we were getting told off, to see the headmaster. They think you should go to school and leave them at school.'

(Parent)

Equally important was the confidence gained from knowing what could be done to help their children at home:

'Well every time I sat down to read with them they didn't take any notice. They were just doing other things. I got a bit 'oh all right they don't do it, fine'. So I just left it and left it and left it. Now he listens to me but he still does what he's doing. If he's playing he's still playing but he's also listening to me as well. If I ask him what I've just told him he won't say anything, he hasn't developed the language yet.'

(Parent)

In one programme where parents had worked on planning and organising time to spend sharing reading with their children, as part of their Wordpower accreditation, they mentioned the impact this had in the family:

'I wouldn't say that it was everyday. I couldn't say that every day, although the reading is every day so you're obviously taking time then but I would say a good three, four times a week, especially at weekends.'

(Female parent)

'I've enjoyed playing with them. Perhaps before it was a way of keeping them busy while I did things, now it's a way of playing with them'.

(Parent)

Parents' learning benefits

Most programmes gave parents the opportunity to improve their basic skills, usually with the possibility of accreditation. In a few examples, there was a stronger focus on children's achievement, with less emphasis on parents' own learning. In these cases, it was assumed that parents' own literacy would improve as a result of becoming more involved in their children's literacy development.

Accreditation

Accreditation of learning in family literacy programmes was one clear outcome in terms of parents' learning, and was available to most parents who took part in family literacy programmes. Some programmes placed a greater emphasis on achieving this objective than others. Although Wordpower Foundation Level was the most frequent form of accreditation of parents' learning, other forms of accreditation, such as Open College were used. In one programme where volunteer tutors were recruited to do individual outreach work with Muslim mothers in the home, accreditation took the form of training to work with the mothers and a City and Guilds qualification.

From the information available to us, around 50% of the parents who attended the 18 programmes studied, achieved accreditation of one sort or another by the time field work had been completed.

Progress in literacy

Only two programmes established clear baseline assessment when parents were recruited. As indicated earlier, adults' competence in literacy on entry to the programme tended to be assessed by informal means. Not all programmes kept formal records of adults' progress: this would not have been appropriate in the case of those which aimed to produce resources or run workshops. Where records were kept they were commendable in terms of the level of detail they contained. Parents' progress tended to be assessed informally, for example through tutor observations of parental ability to communicate within small groups and within the larger group; completion of course-work for accreditation; parents' self-assessment and evaluation; and diary accounts and other records kept by the parents of, among other things, observations of their children.

Parents' perceptions of how they benefited from family literacy

Some parents did not wait to be asked whether they had benefited – they volunteered the information as soon as they started talking about the programme. In terms of helping themselves as learners, similar benefits were mentioned by all parents interviewed. These included better communication in writing, more confidence in speaking and better spelling. Below are some of the comments made by parents about their own progress in learning:

> *'It's helping me to understand things better – when I'm writing things out, how to word them out properly, my own spelling is getting better, communication and confidence. At one time I wouldn't have been able to sit here and talk to you – I'd go red and just clam up and start stammering. So I've got a lot more confidence that way as well.'*
>
> (Parent)

When asked to reflect on the programme and identify the main things that they had achieved, one mother said:

> *'A knowledge of education and an ability to know you can still do it. The knowledge I have a brain and finding myself wanting to do a lot more with myself.'*
>
> (Parent)

Adult participants recognised that involvement in family literacy had not only helped their children's development, but also their own. There was also evidence that they were prepared to learn from their children:

> *'I didn't need help with reading, it was . . . my punctuation and my spelling. I did like a spelling test this afternoon. I got 5 out of 15. I got the meaning of the word but it was like the letters were the wrong way round. It's just my punctuation and my spelling, but it's getting better. Plus I've been on the computer today with the kids, they showed me how to use that. I had an idea but they know better.'*
>
> (Parent)

And with reference to her husband who also attended the course:

'He's more confident in himself, . . . Where before he was like "I can't read, I'm not doing it". But he's. . . more confident in himself, to go on and do, because you know he wouldn't do the reading or the work he brought home, he wouldn't try.'

There were also examples of family literacy helping in specific ways:

'I know I've always had spelling difficulties from being at school. This is my chance to correct it. And I love it'.

(Parent)

In some instances, involvement in family literacy gave parents sufficient confidence and knowledge to be able to register for adult or further education courses held elsewhere. Those interviewed often said that they would never have thought of doing this before their involvement in family literacy.

- In 7 programmes 75% or more of participants continued in some form of education or training, or took up employment.

- In another 6 programmes, at least 50% of parents progressed in some way.

- In 3 programmes, 50% or less progressed to other educational provision or employment

- For the other 2 programmes data was unavailable.

Although not a specific aim of family literacy programmes, continuation in education or training was a clear outcome of many. The degree of take-up of other forms of educational provision depended on a number of factors, firstly whether suitable provision was readily available and accessible. In a few cases, provision was made locally to accommodate those who had completed family literacy programmes. In at least eight programmes parents were helped to identify progression routes into courses offered by further education sector colleges, community education or WEA provision.

It was clear that not only could parents' expectations be raised for their children, but also for themselves. This is an area in which there appeared to be much potential for development between partner agencies, and with good local co-ordination, parents' raised expectations for their own learning could then be met.

Benefits identified by partner agencies

Adult basic skills providers identified being able to reach a new group of adults in need of basic skills provision as the main benefit. Thus, for those involved in Basic Skills work, there were considerable gains. Some even said they saw family literacy as being one of the best innovations for a very long time. The following responses typify the professional benefits felt by adult basic skills tutors:

'I think the difference with family literacy, (is that) it isn't just a mum coming along to a community group for help, it's the fact that she's also valuing education in a much wider context —'

(Adult Basic Skills Tutor)

One tutor identified the difference between existing ways of working in basic skills provision and the commitment required of participants in family literacy:

'Well, I think traditionally, literacy basic skills programmes have tended to be organised so people don't have to expose themselves too publicly. With family literacy, someone's made a fairly solid declaration . . . that they've got a difficulty. It's a much more exposed kind of environment than the traditional delivery of basic skills which allowed the opportunity for people to move away from the locality.'

(Programme Co-ordinator)

This tutor recognised the strengths of family literacy and especially the idea of siting courses within local schools:

'The strength of family literacy is actually in recognising and getting people to come to terms with it in their locality, using the children in the school as the vehicle by which people can begin to reflect upon their own particular needs and providing the vehicle within the locality so people don't have to travel, because one of the other difficulties with traditional provision is if people couldn't or didn't want to travel they didn't access the provision.'

(Programme Co-ordinator)

The involvement of schools in family literacy programmes brought a number of benefits and also some challenges for the future. One of the key benefits was seen as enhanced awareness and understanding of parents and their needs.

'I've had more satisfaction, I think in many respects, from this course than anything I've done for a long while . . . this course has given me a lot of insights. I've learned a lot from the parents, a lot of things that I didn't really realise before. Particularly about the commitment parents are willing to make to help their children.'

(Class Teacher, Primary School)

Where programmes were sited in schools, this meant that programme staff and teachers in school worked together to help build better home-school links. And where this happened, success was likely to follow in terms of the programme's impact on home/school relations. A parent remarked that:

'I used to bring them [the children] to school but I'd never go into their classes. Now we're going in like every afternoon I go in like different classes, with the reading'.

(Parent)

A further benefit from participation in family literacy was in the collaboration between professionals from different phases of education, which often brought opportunities for continuing professional development. Several school teachers working alongside adult basic skills tutors indicated that they had learned new ways of relating to parents as adults in their own right:

> *'I've learned a lot from . . . (the adult basic skills tutor) about how to work with adults; she's excellent, she has such a nice manner with them. I shudder to think how I've treated adults . . . parents in the past, like the children really. This has been a real eye-opener for me about working with parents.'*
>
> (Teacher, Primary School)

In two other programmes based in primary schools, the headteachers and class teachers had been involved in planning the curriculum for adults and had learned about Wordpower accreditation through working jointly with the adult basic skills tutor.

> *'They (school staff) learned that from me as we went along, just as I learned their skills from them as we went along . . . you show somebody a Wordpower assessment book and they look in horror! But I was explaining as I went along, as we were working things out, with the teachers . . .'*
>
> (Programme Co-ordinator)

Some schools admitted that they tended to be rather insular in their assumptions and norms and had to consider how to accommodate programme staff who were not already members of the school. Several basic skills tutors remarked that they had to become accepted and established within schools before they could develop links.

The headteachers and teachers interviewed were aware of the value of family literacy, and especially the fact that the children involved had gained from greater continuity between home and school in literacy development. However, they also acknowledged the work which needed to be done in clarifying the school's role in inter-generational work. There was also an awareness of the new directions which family literacy has presented for primary schools:

> *'It's refreshing for me that schools have been prepared to say "Yes, we'll take on parents too." We need to work with parents and their children. For me that's what family literacy has done, it's brought schools together with adult education tutors, whom we've never met before.'*
> (Headteacher)

In general, other partners had a lower profile than schools and partners responsible for basic skills provision. However, the library service had a key role in many programmes, whether a formal partner or not. As parents became more involved in their children's literacy development more books were required. In programmes which involved the library service this gap was quickly filled by good collaborative working relationships between teachers and librarians. In several programmes in our sample, a library visit was undertaken by parents and children as part of the curriculum; in all of these programmes parents and children joined the local library and started to use it on a regular basis.

It is clear from the information in this chapter that there were a wide range of benefits ensuing from small grants programmes. These related to parents' and children's learning and awareness of the importance of literacy. They also related to the experience gained from working in partnership with other agencies. It is not possible to say that any particular approach to family literacy brought greater benefits than another approach. Measurement of benefits needs to be undertaken over a longer period of time and baseline and final assessment of parents' and children's attainment and progress would need to be kept systematically. At the same time, it is important not to lose sight of the benefits which are less easy to quantify; those which are personal and possibly even subjective.

CHAPTER SEVEN

Material and human factors affecting the success of programmes

THIS chapter identifies the factors which affected the success of programmes. Some of these were material, such as location, timing and resources. However, a key element was the human factor: the staffing and management of each programme.

Location

A notable feature of many of the programmes studied was their location in settings familiar to the children involved. 15 of these programmes were either organised from, or took place within a primary school setting. The remaining 3 programmes were placed in other focal points within the community such as family or adult education centres.

Some programmes were organised and managed from a primary school but took place on more than one site. Sometimes the reasons for this were purely pragmatic. For example, some programmes involved parallel sessions requiring more than one room which proved difficult to obtain in the same building and had to be found elsewhere. In other cases dual or multi-site location was integral to the nature of the programme on offer. This took various forms. In one programme volunteers were trained in the school's community room and, once trained, conducted their tutorial work on a one-to-one basis within individual family homes. The community room continued to be the venue for sessions supporting the volunteers' work within the community. In another two schools, a project was conducted at various venues. The school was usually the starting point for the making of resources (story-sacks) but these were frequently completed by the volunteers at home. Lending libraries and workshops aimed at disseminating the idea of the story-sacks to families took place in various venues throughout the community.

In all cases it appeared that participants', especially the children's, familiarity with the site was a significant factor in a programme's success.

The suitability of a programme's location was also a factor in its success. Some schools which housed programmes already had sufficient space and an appropriate room. Others spent a considerable amount of time, effort and money on ensuring that the space allocated to the programme within the school was suitably attractive to those participating. Criteria for judging the physical surroundings included space, furnishings, safety, access to essential facilities, refreshments, resources and other materials and equipment. Less tangible criteria, requiring a more subjective judgement, included ethos and quality of the welcome given, both of which tended to be enhanced by an attractive comfortable environment with carpets and soft furnishings. According to both sets of criteria, 90% of the venues were classed as suitable by those implementing the programme. Venues were classed as unsuitable for two reasons; lack of space and hostility from the host institution. These two factors were not unrelated.

Materials and other resources

Most programmes had to acquire new resources of one sort or another to enable their family literacy initiative to run as intended. Most common among these were materials used in teaching, monitoring and assessing adult basic skills and books for children. Materials were also required for publicity and for producing other resources such as story-sacks.

A few programmes used part of their grant to buy computer hardware and software, video equipment and tapes, cassette recorders and cassettes which would also be available for subsequent use. School personnel readily admitted that acquiring these additional resources was an added incentive for them to participate in the initiative.

Catering for domestic needs

All programme organisers were conscious of the need to take account of the domestic schedules of participating parents. Nearly a quarter of the children in participating families were under five. In four programmes, crèche facilities were made available to parents where these were not already present locally. Individual sessions were invariably held to coincide with either a full morning or afternoon session at school. This allowed parents to combine attendance in the programme with arrangements for taking and collecting children to and from school.

In one exceptional case, where restrictions on space did not allow the adult and child elements to be housed on the same site, arrangements became more complex and less convenient. In this case the length of individual parent sessions had to be shortened to help overcome the logistical problems which emerged. In several programmes restrictions on the use of shared space and resources sometimes limited the length of joint sessions. In a similar number, which catered for children of school age, disruption to normal classroom routine was avoided or kept to a minimum by shortening the length of joint sessions at times when this was considered the best solution.

Staffing

In the 18 programmes studied, their administration involved a total of 62 partners. The number of partners per programme ranged from two to six with three being the most common. The four most common partners were schools, community education services, local education authorities and further education sector institutions. The emphasis was very firmly on partners with strong educational interests, which appeared significant in terms of keeping the successful programmes 'on track'. There were, however, also a number of successful programmes in which the partners came from other bodies with wider interests, such as local businesses, library services, charities such as the Workers' Educational Association and special initiatives such as City Challenge.

The 18 programmes involved a total of 55 members of staff. The number of staff per programme ranged from one to six with two and three being the most common. Most often, the successful programmes involved adult basic skills tutors from further education sector institutions and school teachers. Slightly less frequently involved were adult basic skills tutors from the community education sector, nursery nurses or Pre-school Playgroup Association workers, and volunteers. It did appear that, for most programmes, staff enthusiasm was vital, but it was not a substitute for special expertise.

Partnership arrangements

In the majority of programmes, the partners responsible for submitting the original proposal to the Basic Skills Agency and the key staff involved in implementing the programme were separate individuals with different roles and responsibilities. There were exceptions to this. In two programmes the key tutors were also involved in writing the proposal for funding. Thus, although we hoped to be able to distinguish between partnerships at a strategic level and those at an operational level, in practice the situation was more complex. Some partners were actively involved at both levels throughout the duration of the programme, others were active only at key points in a programme's development and others still remained either passive or had highly specific inputs. In addition there was considerable variation across programmes both in the numbers of agencies/organisations taking part and in the timing of different partners' periods of activity/inactivity within a programme's development. Whatever the differences both across and within programmes, however, it did emerge that two-way communication between those involved in the collaborative arrangements at the strategic level and those involved in the collaborative arrangements at the operational level was of paramount importance.

Although some programmes developed partnerships at the operational level without having partners in any real sense at the strategic or policy level, and achieved a degree of success in getting the programme going, the value of strong strategic partnership became apparent in the longer term. Some programmes did not seem likely to continue either because strategic partnership or practical support by influential persons was not present. These programmes showed little evidence that they were able to sustain family literacy provision beyond the initial injection of funding. They did not build the idea of continued provision into their area or institution development plans. It would seem then that while strong strategic partnerships were not a necessary condition for success in the shorter term, it may be that in the longer term, partnership and inter-agency co-operation at the strategic level is crucial to ensure and facilitate continuation.

Programme policy and administration

Although the range of partners involved in the programmes was wide, their degree of involvement, and their roles, varied considerably across and within programmes. Whilst most partners were involved in drawing up the proposal to the Agency, not all of them retained an active role throughout. In some cases their involvement was nominal. This was sometimes due to the fact that a partner, though supportive of the idea, did not necessarily see a clear role for their organisation in the administration and operation of the programme.

Various modes of programme administration were observed. In some programmes, managers at the area level took most of the decisions concerning funding, resources and staffing out of the hands of the host institution. At the other extreme, one programme delegated all these decisions to the grassroots level and in the process provided considerable opportunities for indirect staff development.

In some cases administration was complicated because there were several different projects in operation simultaneously, each having its own separate administrative and accountability systems. This level of complexity appeared to hinder the overall success of the programme. By contrast, in another programme, funding from several sources was pooled and allocated via a steering committee set up at area level. This system of management facilitated the administration and accountability by streamlining the paperwork.

The real value of partnerships at the policy level was where provision for family literacy was evident in local strategic planning. This happened sometimes as a result of collegial leadership. In other cases an influential individual or 'key driver' was able to have an impact at area level. The following are examples of the range of management styles observed.

One programme was situated in an area where a number of key people with relevant and substantial experience had come together to form one steering committee with a clearly defined value system and view of the future. In this arrangement, accountability was seen as part of planning. Structures were put in place to ensure that good ideas supported by special grants were quickly and effectively integrated into local communities. This collegial leadership had a long history and drew personnel with status from six different agencies or organisations. Over the years they had learned to share power, authority and resources to achieve their objectives. Some members committed funds and resources in addition to their time and expertise, whereas others were only able to commit their time and expertise. The family literacy initiative was introduced to schools through this existing local structure. Each school was given sufficient incentive in terms of additional resources and support from a specially appointed co-ordinator at area level.

Two programmes, which shared the same co-ordinator, were examples of where a person in the role of 'key-driver' was critical to the success of the initiative at the implementation level. In these two programmes the co-ordinator was an adult educator with wide-ranging previous experience of developmental work related to family literacy. This experience included working with Wordpower as a tutor and verifier, and familiarity with adapting it to a range of situations and client groups. The co-ordinator was instrumental in developing a coherent curriculum for all three elements of family literacy provision as well as liaising with the headteacher and under-five's teacher in two schools. Furthermore, she involved the school staff closely in planning a syllabus mapped to the requirements for Wordpower accreditation and throughout the accreditation process. Although these two programmes ran for only ten weeks each, all the participants who attended the full course achieved Wordpower accreditation.

The co-ordinator of these two programmes was active in seeking a means of continuing family literacy provision after the initial funding period. In this she was successful: the programme continued, and was funded by the Workers' Educational Association, through a grant from the European Social Fund, and by a local further education college. This 'key-driver' was employed by the community education service on a part-time basis. Although she received strong support from the community education centre manager, particularly in seeking continuation funding, there were two structural factors which affected the extent of her role and influence. One of these was the way in which community education was funded in the area, and the second, dependent on the first, was the status of the co-ordinator herself, who was employed on a part-time, hourly paid basis. Clearly, if a strong relationship is to be developed between the management of family literacy at the implementation level and its adoption at strategic policy level, the role and status of the 'key-driver' may need further consideration and a more securely funded post.

In this example, two programmes were funded within the small grants initiative, but were also part of a larger network of family literacy programmes, organised and monitored by the community education service and involving a range of partner agencies. The two included in the sample were both based in primary schools and co-ordinated by a basic skills tutor who was responsible for leading the adult and joint elements of both programmes. In one of the two, the school intended to provide continuation funding for the programme from its own budget for the next academic year. The headteacher of the school recognised the value of family literacy and the contribution made by the co-ordinator in implementing the programme in his school. However, the longer term continuation of the programme remained insecure, despite the best efforts of the co-ordinator and school staff.

Although this programme was to continue in the short-term because of its 'key-driver' at the implementation level, there was no connection to the wider strategic policy intentions in that area. Family literacy was strongly supported by the community education centre manager, who was active in seeking sources of funding, but was not supported at policy level by other partners. Members of the Primary Inspectorate were interviewed and whilst there was a clear interest in developments in family literacy in the area, there was also a confessed lack of awareness of the initiative and its outcomes. One reason was that in one area of the local education authority a move towards unitary authority status was planned for 1997; this would have substantial practical and policy implications for the wider development of and support for family literacy.

Thus an interesting and successful programme was supported within the small grants initiative, which might be sustained in the short-term. However, there were serious doubts about the extent to which the programme would continue or develop in the longer term. This was not because it was unsuccessful at implementation level, but because of particular local circumstances at strategic policy level.

Programme implementation

In order for programmes to run smoothly a range of organisational and management arrangements had to be put in place. These are described below and, where there seemed to be important effects upon programmes' success, these are discussed.

Timing and duration of individual sessions

The length of parent sessions ranged from 1.5 to 4 hours. In three quarters of the programmes studied 2 hours was the preferred length. The length of sessions for children also ranged from 1.5 to 3 hours, and again 2 hours was the preferred option in nearly three quarters of the programmes. The length of joint sessions ranged from 1 hour to 4 hours with 1 hour being the preferred option for two thirds of programmes.

Timing and length of course

All three strands in the programmes ranged in length from 10 weeks to 26 weeks.

The length of the adult component of the course was usually related to external accreditation requirements. Consequently, programmes which were course-orientated tended, by and large, to have clear starting and finishing dates planned in advance. In practice, however, the actual length was sometimes confused by a programme having to be suspended due to poor attendance over the Christmas period or during Eid. Some programmes were lengthened, sometimes at the last minute, by a new injection of funding. Also, it was not unusual for families to join at different points in the course. Thus not all families within any one programme experienced the whole course from start to finish. Issues such as these complicated forward planning and arrangements for accreditation.

The key tutors

Each programme was staffed by key tutors, varying from school teachers to basic skills tutors. While most programmes had a team of at least two key tutors, some had only one.

The range of staff in the programmes was wide and tutors came from various backgrounds. Relevant training and previous experience did not necessarily imply formal training in the teaching of adult basic skills.

Although seven of the programmes used volunteers to assist with the implementation of the programme, only two centred the whole initiative around the recruitment and training of volunteers. In one programme, in a multi-ethnic area, the idea was to recruit people from the community as a means of bridging cultural and linguistic differences between the home and the school. This meant that qualified and experienced personnel were not working directly with target parents. Instead qualified and experienced staff concentrated their resources on training and supporting volunteers to do that job for them.

There were differences in the degree to which volunteer tutors were used and the purposes for which their assistance was used. From evidence observed in the seven programmes using volunteers, there is much potential for using such tutors, if recruited and trained carefully. In particular, the use of volunteer tutors was particularly effective in programmes targeting speakers of languages other than English, where the volunteers knew the community language and had access to social and family networks.

Key tutor working arrangements

In order to create appropriate family literacy provision, the Agency expected tutors to work in partnership with at least one other person from another agency or organisation. In most cases teamwork, aimed at joint planning, implementation and evaluation of programmes, did in fact evolve. This meant that many issues had to be carefully negotiated between those agencies or institutions involved. These issues included practical problems concerning who worked where and how particular tutors should work with families.

Because most programmes were sited in schools, it was the basic skills tutor who was working away from his/her 'home territory'. This called for some rethinking of their professional and practical assumptions. To avoid conflicts, a few basic skills tutors, aware of the differences in priorities and ways of working, were deferential to the school and its norms especially in the early stages of programme implementation.

Most of the learning on how best to handle differences took place indirectly through practice. Good collaboration, where partners learned from each other, happened more readily where the programme had appropriately qualified and experienced staff. Although tutors were appreciative of this indirect opportunity to further their professional development, most, and particularly those without relevant previous experience, said that they would have benefited from some direct input. Thus whilst there was an awareness of, and sensitivity to, different priorities and different ways of working among the basic skills tutors and class teachers, most said they would have benefited from in-service training on how to handle the collaborative venture.

The following areas emerged as important from the analysis of the interview data:

- the role of basic skills tutors in schools; development of strategies to ensure their acceptance by members of the school staff;

- the roles and responsibilities of basic skills tutors whilst working with class teachers in sessions involving children only and in planning for these sessions;

- the roles and responsibilities of class teachers when working alongside basic skills tutors in sessions involving adults and in the planning of those sessions;

- the roles and responsibilities of both basic skills tutors and class teachers in planning and teaching joint sessions involving both parents and children.

In a small minority of programmes, partnerships at the level of implementation did not evolve because adult tutors, inexperienced in matters relating to child education, were left more or less to their own devices. It must be pointed out, however, that where this happened, the adult tutors concerned made a commendable job of running the programme, which helped parents with their own literacy and to be better equipped to help their children's literacy development.

Another issue identified was the need to budget for time spent in joint planning and evaluation. Programmes frequently underestimated the time needed for these activities. This was particularly the case when the different agencies and providers of education were housed on different sites. Planning could only take place when all staff were available. In several programmes the basic skills tutors involved were hourly paid which made it harder to arrange planning meetings.

Strategies for continuing programmes after the initial phase

Almost as soon as family literacy programmes had begun, attention was given to how the initiative could be sustained in the longer-term. A key objective for many small-scale programmes was to find alternative sources of funding to replace that provided by the Basic Skills Agency. At least three of the programmes were part of a larger local initiative which had already made provision for continuation funding. Other smaller-scale programmes, particularly those supported by schools which had responsibility for their own budget, were pessimistic about the likelihood of being able to offer financial support to family literacy in the longer-term. We have already indicated the considerable challenges faced by some very effective programmes in finding continuation funding for family literacy in the longer term.

It was clear that partnership arrangements which worked well in relation to getting programmes started and running effectively, needed to be carried through to a level which could influence policy both in individual agencies and strategically. Clear channels of communication and information exchange needed to be established between those responsible for programme implementation at a day-to-day level and those responsible for strategic financial decision making. In only one or two programmes was this evident. Most, if not all, staff responsible for programme implementation were aware of the importance of such channels and did much to draw attention to the family literacy initiative. Structural organisation and arrangements within and between agencies often made this problematic or ineffective in practice.

The small grants initiative provided the stimulus for the development of lasting inter-agency co-operation. Some providers saw this as an opportunity, and grasped it; others saw the value but did not seem to have a clear idea about how to proceed after initial funding came to an end.

Costs

In this we section indicate the cost of running the 18 programmes.

• The total cost of running all 18 programmes was £109,084.24.

• £49,429.16 of this total was met nationally, through funding from the Basic Skills Agency.

• £59,655.08 was funded locally – mostly from partner agencies.

The level of funding provided by the Basic Skills Agency varied substantially across the 18 programmes, depending on the amount applied for:

• 8 programmes received between £500 and £2,000

• 6 received between £3,000 and £3,999

• 3 received £4,000-£5,000

• 1 received less than £500.

The most substantial cost was staffing of programmes

Overall, 70% of funding was spent on staff costs; the rest was spent on materials, travel and ensuring that premises were suitable.

It was not possible to calculate the cost per participant per hour of learning. This was because most programmes continued in one form or another beyond their official finishing date as more funding became available and/or as adult participants needed further support to complete the accreditation requirements. As some programmes were not presented as courses, 'hours of learning' was an inappropriate measure for these.

The costs appear to be evenly divided between local partners and central funding. However, in practice, there were often significant hidden costs related to running a programme, for example in terms of space, time and resources. Most notable among these was the considerable amount of time given by basic skills tutors and class teachers, in addition to their official teaching hours, in order to meet, plan, develop and evaluate the programmes. Yet in few examples were these costs written into a programme's budget. Thus all programmes relied, some to a greater extent than others, on the goodwill and interest of their key staff.

CHAPTER EIGHT

Major lessons and implications arising from the small grants initiative

W E indicated in Chapter 2 that the purpose of the small grants initiative was to develop local work in family literacy. Beyond requiring that each programme aimed to enhance literacy and involved parents and their children with literacy learning, the Basic Skills Agency deliberately allowed scope for diverse forms of provision and organisation. This was in contrast to the demonstration programmes which worked to a clearly specified model. In this chapter, we give an indication of the approaches developed within the small grants scheme which seemed to offer most potential for future development and consider some of the practical lessons emerging from the research.

Did any approach to family literacy work best?

Although the demonstration programmes worked to a specific model of family literacy which was highly effective (Brooks et al. 1996), our research on the small grants initiative indicates that the notion of a model, to be specified in advance and capable of being replicated in a new set of circumstances, was not the most appropriate way of thinking about the provision developed within the small grants scheme. Instead of attempting to specify a model or models, we have identified particular approaches to family literacy which seem to be effective and can be sustained locally.

One approach to local work in family literacy closely paralleled the demonstration programme model, with some modifications. In two very effective examples of this approach, provision was offered for one half day a week for ten weeks, based in two local infant schools. There were separate sessions for parents and children and joint sessions where both worked together. The programmes were staffed by an adult basic skills tutor and an early years teacher. The content of the parents' and joint sessions was matched to the accreditation requirements of Wordpower Foundation Level. These programmes showed that the demonstration programme model can be used effectively with relatively small amounts of funding in local contexts. However, there are some lessons which emerged in relation to ensuring that this approach would work equally effectively elsewhere. These included:

- A clear understanding of the aims of intergenerational family literacy and the contribution it can make to children's and parents' learning in literacy.

- Previous joint development work between the school and adult education providers. In this case the community education service had a substantial track record of joint work with schools in the area. The two infant schools involved had staff with expertise and experience in early years curriculum development.

- Staff who were appropriately trained and had substantial relevant experience, and enthusiasm for making family literacy work.

- Flexibility and willingness on the part of adult basic skills tutors and early years teachers to work in new ways and to learn from each other.

- Strong and active support from line managers (school headteachers and the community education centre manager) for the programme and its staff.

- Careful and detailed planning by the adult basic skills tutor and early years teacher of all three strands of family literacy to ensure coherence and consistency between the parents', children's and joint sessions and to match session content to accreditation requirements.

The approach outlined above, which closely paralleled the demonstration programme model in making provision for children, for parents and for joint work, appeared to work best where both schools (or other early childhood education providers) had already worked together and developed an understanding of how each could make both an individual and collaborative contribution to family literacy. If such previous work had not already been undertaken, either investment would need to be made in development work, or possibly another approach to family literacy would need to be taken in the initial stages.

Lessons from the small grants programmes

In this section we summarise the main lessons emerging from the small grants initiative.

Lessons related to the content and teaching approaches of family literacy programmes:

1. Well-planned joint parent child sessions were central to successful examples of family literacy work, whatever the specific approach taken by the programme.

2. Time for parents to prepare for the joint sessions with their children, and to 'rehearse' and discuss with each other particular tasks to be done later with children, was an important factor in the success of programmes. The connection between the joint and separate sessions was particularly important for the adult participants.

3. The content of successful sessions related to the everyday lives of parents and children, but also offered ample opportunities for parents to discuss and reflect on their experience past and present.

4. Tutors' skill in using adults' experience as parents or learners as a focus for the activity or topic made an important contribution to successful adult sessions. Adults were interested in knowing more about their children's learning and in reflecting on their own experience as learners.

5. A key element in the success of the adult sessions was the way in which adult basic skills tutors fostered a positive and cohesive atmosphere within groups, offering encouragement to complete work for accreditation. Many parents were apprehensive about returning to learning and were lacking in confidence at the beginning of the programme.

6. The advantage of programmes which offered continuous courses was that motivation and peer support were easier to maintain.

Working with bilingual families

7. A number of bilingual parents admitted that, had the opportunity to become more involved in their child's education not been presented to them through a family literacy programme, they would probably not have sought it out for themselves.

8. Programmes working with a specific group of bilingual parents benefited from the involvement of a tutor who spoke the dominant community language.

9. The training of volunteers who spoke a relevant community language was a successful way of working with speakers of languages other than English, particularly where there was some home delivery of family literacy.

10. A parent/child model of the family may be too narrow in some communities. The notion of family needed to be flexible and inclusive where programmes aimed to work with ethnic minority families. For example, some programmes worked effectively with elder siblings and other family members.

Work with children

11. A specialist early childhood education input was essential for planning and delivering high quality work with pre-school age children. This expertise took various forms, including school staff, nursery nurses and pre-school playgroup association staff.

12. Appropriate provision for school-age children within a family literacy programme needs careful planning and liaison between the school and the family literacy staff.

13. Early years teachers in schools and nurseries need to be convinced of the value of dedicating time to family literacy which may also take them away from their role with a whole class.

14. When based in a school, family literacy needs to have a high profile within the institution, with all staff understanding and supporting its aims and objectives.

Assessment and progression

15. Adults appreciated the opportunity for accreditation. They were often pleasantly surprised at how their work was assessed, for example within Wordpower. Many adults gained greater confidence from being involved in continuous assessment and in constructing portfolios of work.

16. An additional outcome in many small grants programmes was the progression of adults into other forms of learning. Even those who were not able to progress often indicated an increased interest in further education take-up.

17. Only two programmes established clear baseline assessment when parents were recruited. Adult competence in literacy on entry to the programme tended to be assessed by informal means.

18. Parents' progress also tended to be assessed informally, for example through tutor observations of parental ability to communicate within small groups and within the larger group; completion of course-work for accreditation; parents' self-assessment and evaluation; and diary accounts and other records kept by the parents of, among other things, observations of their children.

19. A limitation of using informal means of assessment was that progress could not be quantified, for the benefit of either programme staff or parents. Similar limitations were noted where children's progress was assessed informally. Programmes might consider how sympathetic but rigorous baseline and progressive assessment techniques might be developed within small-scale family literacy programmes.

Recruitment and retention of participants

20. Underlying all the examples of successful recruitment was a careful needs analysis in the communities which family literacy was aiming to serve. Programme staff spent a considerable amount of time and effort identifying and making contact with potential participants, before the programme began. In some cases, this was done prior to publicising family literacy.

21. Approaching suitable parents through informal personal contact was an effective way to reach them. Schools had a key role to play in this respect. Conversations with parents when they brought or collected children to and from school were one way of making contact. 'Taster sessions' or open days, such as coffee mornings or demonstrations of aspects of family literacy were also effective ways of attracting parents.

22. Printed materials such as posters or flyers advertising family literacy were most effectively used as a back up for personal contact.

23. Less effective ways of recruiting suitable parents were through sending letters or publicity materials 'cold' to homes. The parents attracted by such publicity tended to be those who were already able to support their children and had little need of help with their own basic skills.

24. It did not always follow that parents keen to participate in schemes to help their children had poor basic skills, or that those who had poor basic skills would automatically identify family literacy as being appropriate to their needs. Programme staff had to maintain a delicate balance between ensuring that courses and workshops were well-subscribed, and ensuring that parents who did participate were those who would themselves benefit from family literacy.

25. The close match between need, as perceived by programme organisers, and parents' actual desire to participate, was critical to success in recruiting and retaining a cohort of participants.

26. There was a difference in the level of success experienced by those programmes which deliberately targeted 'hard to reach' parents whose basic skills needs were acute, but who were reluctant to participate in educational activities, or even groups.

27. There was evidence to suggest that 'hard to reach parents', with very poor basic skills and social confidence, could be reached more effectively at a later stage in programme development. A particularly effective way of encouraging them to come forward was through personal contact with parents who had been successfully involved in family literacy.

28. Previous experience in recruiting similar groups of adults for basic skills courses, or other related work, was helpful in identifying the best ways to publicise family literacy. Developing and sharing expertise in appropriate recruitment strategies was one aspect in which inter-agency collaboration was particularly important.

29. Even those programmes which had staff with substantial experience of recruiting adults for purposes relevant to family literacy had to adapt to new circumstances. For example, partners with successful experience of recruiting parents for school parental involvement schemes, had to learn how to encourage parents with poor basic skills to return to learning.

30. It did not appear to make a difference whether or not programmes used the specific title *family literacy* in their publicity material, or whether another name was used. What was important in successful recruitment of appropriate parents was that at some stage in the recruitment process the aims of family literacy and its three dimensions were made clear to parents. It was apparent that programmes which had been clear about this aspect of family literacy provision avoided misunderstandings at a later stage in the programme. However, there was no easy solution to the challenge of recruiting parents with poor basic skills.

Retention of participants

31. Reasons for high levels of retention were not always related to programme factors. For example in one programme which recruited eight suitable parents, two dropped out: one because of the death of a close family member and another because she got a job.

32. Highly stressful family problems, of considerable severity, were often the cause of poor or sporadic attendance. In some cases individuals ceased to attend for a considerable period of time, but returned as soon as they were able. Other programmes had a fluctuating population of attendees – some dropped out but were replaced by others who wanted to join the programme after the initial start date.

33. There was little connection between retention and the length or structure of programmes.

The organisation, management and staffing of family literacy

Location

34. A notable feature of many of the programmes was their location in settings familiar to the children involved. 15 of these programmes were either organised from, or took place within a primary school setting.

35. Primary schools were usually easily accessible to parents whose children already attended that school. The provision of transport to and from a centre offered a way to encourage participants who did not have easy access to the family literacy programme.

36. The suitability of a programme's location was a factor in its success. Most programmes spent a considerable amount of time, effort and money on ensuring that the space allocated to the programme within the school was suitably attractive to those participating.

37. The provision of crèche facilities was made by some programmes: one creatively used BTEC nursery nurse students within the partner further education college to this end.

Timing

38. Individual sessions were frequently held to coincide with either a full morning or afternoon session at school. This allowed parents to combine attendance in the programme with arrangements for taking and collecting children to and from school.

39. The preferred total length of the majority of programmes was 2 hours a week. The length of individual child sessions also ranged from 1.5 to 3 hours, and again 2 hours was the preferred option in nearly three quarters of the programmes. The length of individual joint sessions ranged from 1 hour to 4 hours with 1 hour being the preferred option for two thirds of programmes.

Staffing

40. Most programmes involved both staff with adult basic skills experience and those with teaching experience appropriate to the age of the children involved. The involvement of appropriately qualified and experienced staff was an important positive factor in the success of small grants programmes. However, a small number of staff with alternative qualifications and experience, complementary to family literacy, made a strong contribution to the success of individual programmes. However, overall, enthusiasm was not a substitute for appropriate training and experience.

41. The inter-change of ideas, joint planning and sharing of expertise between staff was an important element in the successful implementation of family literacy. Several successful programmes indicated that they had not built in and budgeted for enough time for staff to plan jointly. A very clear lesson for future programmes was apparent here.

42. Because most programmes were sited in schools, it was the basic skills tutor who was working away from his/her 'home territory'. Schools needed to be alert and sensitive to the situation. They also needed to ensure that family literacy staff not based in the school were made welcome and knew the protocol of the institution in which they were temporarily working.

85

43. Good collaboration, where partners learned from each other, happened more readily where the programme had appropriately qualified and experienced staff. Most of the learning on how best to handle differences took place indirectly through practice. Whilst there was an awareness of, and sensitivity to, different priorities and different ways of working among the basic skills tutors and class teachers, most said they would have benefited from in-service training on how to handle the collaborative venture.

Partnership arrangements

44. The emphasis was very firmly on partners with strong educational interests, which appeared significant in terms of keeping the successful programmes 'on track'. There were also a number of successful programmes in which the partners came from other bodies with wider interests, such as local businesses, library services, charities such as the Workers' Educational Association and special initiatives such as City Challenge.

Programme management

45. Two-way communication between those involved in the collaborative arrangements at the strategic level and those involved in the collaborative arrangements at the operational level was of paramount importance.

46. While strong strategic partnerships were not a necessary condition for success in the shorter term, it may be that in the longer term partnership and inter-agency co-operation at the strategic level is crucial to ensure and facilitate continuation.

47. If a strong relationship is to be developed between the management of family literacy at the implementation level and its adoption at strategic policy level, the role and status of the programme's 'key-driver' may need careful consideration and a securely funded post.

48. Some programmes did not seem likely to continue either because strategic partnership or practical support by influential persons was not present. These programmes showed little evidence that they were able to sustain family literacy provision beyond the initial injection of funding. They did not build the idea of continued provision into their area or institution development plans.

References

ALBSU (1993) *Parents and Their Children: The Intergenerational Effects of Poor Basic Skills.* London: ALBSU.

Brooks, G., Gorman, T., Harman. J., Hutchinson, D., Wilkin. A. (1996) *Family Literacy Works.* London: Basic Skills Agency.

Francis, H. (1994) 'Literacy – the role of the family' *Viewpoints 15,* 1994. ALBSU 9-12.

Hannon, P. (1995) *Literacy, Home and School.* London: Falmer Press.

National Assessment of Educational Progress (1991) *The 1989-90 National Assessment of Reading and Literature.* Denver: NAEP.

Ryan, K.E., Geissler, B., Knell, S. (1994) 'Evaluating Family Literacy Programmes: Tales from the Field' in Dickinson, D.K. *Bridges to Literacy.* Oxford: Basil Blackwell.

St. Pierre, R., Layzer, J. and Barnes, H. (1994) *Variation in the design, cost, and effectiveness of two-generation programs.* Paper presented at Eighth Rutgers Invitational Symposium on Education: New Directions for Policy and Research in Early Childhood Care and Education, Princeton, NJ, October 27-28.

Sticht, T., Beeler, M., and McDonald, B. (1992) *The Intergenerational Transfer of Cognitive Skills.* New Jersey: Ablex.

Tizard, J., Schofield, W.N., Hewison, J. (1982) 'Collaboration Between Teachers and Parents in Assisting Children's Reading'. *British Journal of Educational Psychology.* Vol 52, pp 1-15.

Topping, K and Wolfendale, S. (1985) (Eds) *Parental Involvement in Children's Reading.* London: Croom Helm.

Aims, methodology and planned outcomes/benefits of programmes sampled[1]

Programme 1

Background

This programme was a single-site initiative, located in a school which had a 99% intake of Muslim children whose mother-tongue was a language other than English. Some of the mothers had limited collaboration with the school because they were in Purdah. Thus, on entry into school, for cultural and linguistic reasons, the opportunities for bridging home and school literacies were limited. The key purpose of introducing the family literacy programme was to tackle this problem by deliberately targeting the mothers (in Purdah) of children who were attending the school's nursery and reception classes.

The school had a long history of good community relations and had easy access to a number of professionals from different education services and other agencies with substantial previous experience of running family-orientated, community-based programmes. The family literacy programme was planned and managed strategically and operationally by the reception class teacher who acted as the administrator/manager. She was supported by a specially arranged steering committee made up of representatives from the three partners involved – the school, the local college and the local community education team.

---

1. Since many of the programmes had not finished when the research ended, we cannot give data on a programme by programme basis on the extent to which planned outcomes were achieved.

Aims

- to create a network of support and guidance between the home and the school

- to encourage parents and children to work on reading and writing together

- to develop a reading and communication programme within the home environment as a means of bridging home and school literacies.

Methodology

1. To recruit and train 10 volunteer tutors and provide a programme of staff development through liaison with different agencies within the community.

2. To use the following criteria to select volunteer tutors and to relate these criteria to City and Guilds Initial Certificate in Teaching Basic Skills (9284):

   - ability to speak the mother tongue in order to support the work in the home aimed at creating a positive learning environment

   - competence at a functional level in English

   - potential to learn how to (a) assess and identify learners' needs (b) design and deliver a learning programme (c) select and adapt suitable resources (d) evaluate learning.

3. To include the following in the training programme for volunteers:

   - familiarity with school methods of teaching literacy in the early years

   - encourage independence and confidence in different learning contexts drawing on elements of City and Guilds 3793 Wordpower Foundation Level

   - help each learner to achieve meaningful targets within the above accreditation with particular emphasis on reading and speaking in everyday social contexts.

4. To appoint a co-ordinator to the project who will have the dual responsibility of the co-ordination and training of the volunteers.

5. To provide a suitable room with appropriate facilities within the school for training to take place.

6. To sensitively match each of the volunteer tutors with a targeted mother in Purdah whom they will be visiting and coaching at home along the lines outlined above for one session each week.

Planned Outcomes/Benefits

- tangible outcomes measured in terms of numbers (volunteer tutors and mothers in Purdah) recruited, retained, and accredited

- increased interaction in learning situations between targeted mothers and their children

- increased confidence among targeted mothers and their children enabling them to participate more frequently and more effectively in school activities

- evidence of a two-way learning process between home and school.

Programme 2

Background

This programme was one part of a multi-site family literacy initiative. The intention at area level was to pilot the idea in six carefully chosen schools.

The school which housed the one programme sampled was situated on a large council estate where the population was largely Caucasian. It served an area where there was reputed to be a history of poor social integration and slow communication development among the children. This reputation was based on a mixture of official statistics for employment, health and educational attainment, all indicating an area of considerable deprivation, and the perceptions of outsiders of the community. In the years immediately prior to the programme the school had developed good relationships with the parent constituency and the wider community. This work had been enhanced by the appointment of a home-school liaison teacher.

The area-wide initiative was managed by a steering committee made up of key people with relevant and substantial experience. This steering committee, representing six different agencies, had been in existence for a number of years and had managed similar initiatives in the past. At institutional level a class teacher was designated to take charge of the project and co-ordinate it within the school as well as being directly involved in the planning and implementation of elements of the programme. At area level a co-ordinator was specially appointed to act as broker for the steering committee and the schools involved.

Aims

- to help parents improve their life and parenting skills

- to help parents and children improve their literacy skills

- to set up and resource a suitable room within the school to accommodate parents

- to give staff and parents the 9282/3/4/5 accreditation in working with adults.

Methodology

1. To recruit 10 families to attend a 10-week course with separate two-hour sessions for children and their parents running concurrently, followed by a one-hour joint parent and children session.

2. To include in the course workshops, visits and talks from outside agencies with specialist information.

3. To ensure that the separate parent and child sessions complement each other by involving the same core skills (e.g. using books and newspapers in the home) and incorporating these into the joint sessions.

4. To involve the headteacher and the school's special needs co-ordinator in the sessions as appropriate.

5. To offer accreditation to parents in the form of City and Guilds Wordpower certificates and opportunities to continue their learning through the further development of existing adult education opportunities on site.

6. To support the parents to produce a booklet as a resource for other parents.

7. To recruit members of the school staff and more able parents to attend college to achieve the 9382/3/4/5 accreditation certificates.

8. To accommodate the child sessions in a classroom and the hall, the joint sessions in the hall and the adult sessions in the parents' room.

Planned Outcomes/Benefits

- tangible outcomes measured in terms of numbers (volunteer parents and staff and mothers targeted) recruited, retained, and accredited

- improvement in communication between parents and children and between parents and the school

- usefulness of the family information booklet to other parents

- demonstrate that a pattern of parental involvement and adult training be set in train using a well equipped parents' room.

Programme 3

Background

This was a single-site programme initiated by the local community education team which set out to pilot family literacy in a school within the area which had an established record of good community relations.

The school which housed the programme was situated on a large council estate where the population was largely Caucasian. It served an area where there was reputed to be a history of poor social integration and slow communication development among the children. This reputation was based on a mixture of official statistics for employment, health and educational attainment, all indicating an area of considerable deprivation, and the perceptions of outsiders to the community.

The key purpose of this programme was to intervene in families at the point of entry into the reception class. Whilst all parents of the children attending the nursery class prior to entry into the reception class would be approached, special efforts would be made to recruit the parents whose children had been assessed as having significant language delays.

The programme was planned, managed and implemented by a home-school liaison teacher who was assisted by an adult basic skills tutor. Both were members of the community education team and together had substantial previous experience of running parental involvement and community-based programmes.

Aims

- to encourage reception class parents to recognise and value their key role in preparing their children for reading and in enabling their child to read

- to provide guidance and support for parents with literacy needs to access adult literacy programmes

- to provide an Open College accreditation for the parents

- to enhance the children's language capabilities.

Methodology

1. To assess all children in the nursery class for language delay in the term prior to entry into the reception class.

2. To recruit in the first instance, through home visits, the parents of the children showing significant language delay to attend a 10-week reading workshop course at the school. While all reception class parents would be invited to join, realistically the intention was to cater for a maximum of 12 parents.

3. To staff the reading workshops with a home-school teacher supported by an adult literacy tutor, both from the community team. While the parent workshops were in progress the children would attend the reception class as usual. A crèche would be provided for the children who were too young to attend the nursery class within the school. The ideas developed in the workshops would be tried out immediately in joint sessions with the children. For these joint sessions the children would be released from their normal classroom.

Planned Outcomes/Benefits

- tangible outcomes measured in terms of numbers recruited, retained, and accredited

- demonstrate discernible improvements in children's language development by re-testing the children at the end of the course

- disseminate useful information about this pilot phase of family literacy to other workers in the area.

Programme 4

Background

This programme was part of an area initiative involving several schools. The whole initiative was co-ordinated, managed and evaluated by an advisory teacher who constructed the strategic plans and aims and then acted as broker for funding for individual programmes within local schools.

The school which housed the programme sampled was situated on a large council estate built in the 1930s and, as the only RC primary school in the locality, it drew its children from a relatively wide socially mixed geographical area. A small percentage of the children attending the school were Afro-Caribbean, the others were largely Caucasian.

Aims

- to break the cycle of low attainment and failure that parents with low literacy skills can pass on to their children

- to raise the levels of children's literacy on entry to the nursery

- to empower parents to improve their own literacy skills

- to promote the involvement of fathers in the programme as role models to sons.

Methodology

1. To recruit, using posters, circulars, word of mouth and a specially arranged parents' meeting, 6 families, with children still too young to attend the nursery class, to attend a 10-week family literacy course at the school.

2. To plan and deliver a course for these parents and their children which would be made up of two separate sessions for parents and

toddlers running concurrently, followed immediately by a joint session. These sessions to take place once a week within the school and extend for a full morning (9 am to 12 noon).

3. To staff the adult and joint sessions using a specially appointed adult literacy worker and the child sessions using the nursery nurse from the school's nursery class. All sessions to be supported by the head teacher and, on occasions, by the nursery teacher.

4. To focus the parent sessions on (a) family literacy activities such as story-telling, book-making, finger puppets and (b) support to develop their own literacy skills and increase their self-worth.

Planned Outcomes/Benefits

- tangible outcomes measured in terms of numbers recruited, retained, and accredited

- improved performance among the children entering the nursery class from the toddlers' group and particularly increased engagement with story and book handling skills

- parents enhance their literacy skills so they can apply them effectively in different social and learning contexts

- increased membership of local library by both parents and children.

Programmes 5 and 6

Background

These two programmes were part of an area-wide initiative involving several schools. The whole initiative was managed and co-ordinated by the Principal Community Education Officer (schools). While all individual programmes within the initiative adhered to certain key principles regarding recruitment of the target group and course structure, the scheme was deliberately kept flexible to allow each programme to develop differently in accordance with local needs and conditions.

The two schools which housed programmes 5 and 6 provided examples of contrasting communities and together were representative of the population pattern within the whole local initiative. The school which housed programme 5 had a 97% Muslim intake, whereas the school which housed programme 6 had a 99% Caucasian intake. Each school had good community relations and was assisted in this work by the appointment of a home-school liaison teacher/community worker. Both schools had sufficient space to house the project with relative ease.

Aims

- to increase parents' and children's fluency in English (programme 5 only)

- to increase parents' understanding of how children learn to read and encourage their involvement in the process (programmes 5 and 6)

- to give children access to good exciting books to share with parents as a means of encouraging literacy (programmes 5 and 6)

- to provide a programme within a crèche aimed at developing early literacy skills (programmes 5 and 6).

Methodology

1. To develop a 20 week course for parents which had one session, one and a half hours per week. These sessions were to be run on an individualised basis with a negotiated curriculum and were to be followed immediately by a joint parent-child half-hour session in which the parents and children were to be encouraged to read together. The parents only session planned to include an element which would train parents in how to make the joint sessions useful and enjoyable (programmes 5 and 6).

2. To organise some joint parent and teacher sessions/workshops aimed at sharing ideas about how children learn to read and how parents and teachers can complement each other's work (programmes 5 and 6).

3. To staff the course using an adult education tutor as the key person who would work in close liaison with the class teachers, crèche leader and, in the case of programme 5, the bi-lingual home-school liaison worker. Also, where appropriate, to involve the children's librarian to provide extra books and to act as a role model for story telling (programmes 5 and 6).

Planned Outcomes/Benefits

Increased literacy in English for both parents and children. For the parents in programme 5 this would be evidenced in the parents' ability to communicate in English sufficiently well to communicate with the class teacher and participate in their children's education. Programme 6 would also look for evidence of increased parent-teacher contact in relation to children's learning.

Where appropriate accreditation will be possible through City and Guilds Wordpower or the Open College (programmes 5 and 6).

For children, an increase in the speaking and book-sharing activities (programmes 5 and 6).

Evidence of a lasting partnership developed between school, parents and children (programmes 5 and 6).

Programmes 7 and 8

Background

This was an area-wide initiative involving a scheme which has become known as storysacks. A storysack is a cloth bag or sack containing a story and relevant support materials. These sacks were made by parents for use by parents and children. The storysack idea was the brainchild of the headteacher of the school which housed programme 8. This headteacher managed the project within his own school assisted by the reception class teacher and, additionally, acted as a key driver to spread the project upwards and outwards by bringing in other agencies and schools. This involved setting up a two-tier steering committee to manage the wider project locally. Programme 7 was housed in one of the schools which had been brought into this wider initiative, and, as the two headteachers had worked collaboratively in the past, the project's main ideas were quickly assimilated into this new school.

The two schools housing programmes 7 and 8 served contrasting Caucasian communities. Programme 8 was located in the middle of a recent development of private housing which would by most definitions be regarded as an estate which housed mainly upwardly mobile families. On the other hand, programme 7 was located in the middle of an area where there was reputed to be a history of poor social integration and slow communication development among the children. This reputation was based on a mixture of official statistics for employment, health and educational attainment, all indicating an area of considerable deprivation, and the perceptions of outsiders to the community. This latter programme was managed within the school by the special needs teacher who shared her time between the infant school where the programme was housed and the junior school next door. She was assisted in her work by an ABE tutor from the local college.

Aims

- to enhance the literacy of families by providing good reading and language material and guidance for their use through workshops.

Methodology

1. To recruit, in the first instance, parents willing to give their time to make up the contents of a storysack (programmes 7 and 8).

2. To produce 100 storysacks (programme 8) and 50 (programme 7). Each bag to include one quality children's book together with a range of materials that would bring the book to life.

3. To set up a lending library system for the storysacks to make them available on loan to members of the school community (programmes 7 and 8).

4. To provide workshops as appropriate on how to use these storysacks to promote literacy development (programmes 7 and 8).

Planned Outcomes/Benefits

- to disseminate the storysack locally and beyond (programmes 7 and 8)

- to monitor the storysack as an instrument for raising the literacy standards of children and their parents and as a means of enhancing book-sharing and related activities among parents and their children (programmes 7 and 8).

Programme 9

Background

This programme was situated in a rural area in England, in an area identified as having high levels of unemployment and other indicators of social deprivation. The programme was located on three sites. One aspect of the joint provision for parents and children was located in an infant school as a development from existing work on home/school relations.

Aims

- to improve the literacy skills of under-educated parents and their children, focusing on parents of children preparing to start school in the coming year and in the first year of school

- to establish a model of good practice in family literacy.

101

Methodology

1. To raise awareness of the project through promotional activities, parents' evenings and contact with referral agencies.

2. Run three parallel sessions for families with pre-school children

   • one for parents with limited literacy skills

   • one for the children of these parents

   • joint parent and children sessions.

3. Sessions to be staffed by:

   • ABE tutor (community education)

   • PPA – trained tutor employed by the programme

   • infant/reception class teacher.

Planned Outcomes/Benefits

• to reach over 100 families through awareness raising

• to reach 30 families with limited literacy skills (80% to achieve measurable improvement in skills; 60% evidence of achievement towards a Wordpower certificate).

• to involve 40 children (80% to achieve measurable improvement in skills and social integration; 60% evidence of improvement on early assessment record logged by parents).

Programme 10

Background

This programme was situated in a town in the south of England. It was located in a primary school on a large housing estate on the edge of the town, serving a population with a high level of unemployment and other indicators of economic poverty. The programme had been originally designed as a partnership between a community tenants' association, a secondary school and the FE college's ABE Learning Support Unit; it was intended to be held in the community centre. Factors within the community had necessitated a revision of the original plan; the programme was relocated in the neighbourhood junior school, with that school as an active partner. The programme and the collaborative partnership was a new area of development for the school, and working in a junior school, a new development for the ABE learning support staff.

Aims

The aims of the original proposal were substantially revised in programme implementation to take account of changed local circumstances. However, the overall aim remained unchanged:

- to improve the literacy skills of children and parents in X estate in the community in a family setting.

Methodology

Parents of children in Year 7 at the local secondary school were targeted (this was later changed to parents of children in the feeder junior school). Initially, provision was made for adults through home-based delivery; ABE tutors gave one-to-one tuition to parents who had low levels of achievement in reading and writing. The level of support needed initially by these parents precluded holding group sessions for adults. At a later stage of development, parents came into the junior school for sessions with ABE staff. Separate provision was made for the children by ABE tutors working with the class teacher to provide support. At a later stage in the programme, joint work was developed with parents and children: a video was made of one parent reading with her child in the school; parents joined their children in the classroom to focus on a project on the local community.

Intended outcomes

- recruitment of parents of children in X school with literacy learning needs in order to help them in improving their own basic skills

- development of closer links between the school and community

- improvement in targeted parents' and children's reading, writing and oral communication

- eventual take-up by parents of provision in learning support unit of FE College.

Programmes 11 & 12

Background

These two programmes were situated in South Wales in an urban area with high levels of unemployment. There was a strong tradition of community and adult education in the area; the family literacy programme had been developed from previous collaborations between the community education centre and local schools. More specifically, parents' groups had been organised in a number of primary schools as part of the work of community education. The ABE tutor who co-ordinated the family literacy programme had experience setting up and working with such parents' groups.

Aims

The programme sought to provide parents with a comprehensive grounding in all aspects of basic communication skills, with accreditation. Children were to benefit directly from parents' knowledge and abilities in basic skills. The programme aimed to help parents become familiar with and support children's literacy development and aspects of school life and learning at reception class level. The programme was intended to form a foundation for future work.

Methodology

The programme ran on two sites (both infant schools) and consisted of 10 week courses of two hours. The programme covered reading, writing and oral communication. All aspects of the programme were analysed for basic skills content and related to adult learning and accreditation. The programme was staffed by an ABE tutor (community education), an early years specialist in each school and administrative support was provided by the community education centre.

Intended Outcomes

- 8 adults (maximum) recruited to each 10 week programme (the number of children depended on parents recruited (8 minimum))

- increased parental literacy and communication ability and awareness of children's needs and the school environment

- achievement of accreditation for learning and an increase in parental confidence and raised self-esteem

- increase in children's literacy and communication abilities

- increased motivation towards learning and increased confidence and self-esteem.

Programme 13

Background

This programme was one of several in which the large tertiary college in a city was a partner. The programmes all drew upon existing staff and resources within the college to make provision for a range of local needs. The work undertaken in this programme was supported by previous developments undertaken by the staff responsible and aimed to reach a wide range of parents throughout the city over the period of time for which the programme ran. Its specific focus was reaching parents with basic skills needs who identified themselves as dyslexic.

Aims

To support dyslexic parents and their children; to increase awareness of how to support children with learning difficulties; to help parents access appropriate support and help for their own and their children's learning difficulties.

Methodology

The staff involved in this programme (basic skills tutors from two of the college's sites in the city) ran four, five week programmes at different college sites across the city. Workshops and presentations were held with presentations from experts in areas of learning difficulty and dyslexia. Some of the programme sessions were used for counselling individual parents on how they might access help and support for themselves and their children. The weekly sessions tended to be divided into two parts: one in which there was an input from staff or outside speakers on the learning difficulties of adults and children and the other where parents were involved in practical workshops on strategies for supporting and helping themselves and their children.

Intended outcomes

To achieve the aims; to establish a network of support for parents with learning difficulties and their children across the city. To reach 40-60 parents with learning difficulties during the programme's duration.

Programme 14

Background

This programme was one of several in which the large tertiary college in a city was a partner. The programmes all drew upon existing staff and resources within the college to make provision for a range of local needs. The work undertaken in this programme was supported by previous developments undertaken by the staff responsible and was aimed at a specific population: an ethnic minority community in which there were a number of refugee families. The programme developed from previous work in this community which supported the aims of family literacy.

Aims

To support and enhance the language and communication of refugee parents and children in a particular bilingual community in the city. To increase communication and understanding between parents and their children's schools. To produce reading materials for children to use in school from transcribed and translated oral stories from the community language. To provide ESOL support for parents and other family members (elder siblings of children in primary school).

Methodology

The programme was delivered by a member of staff at the college who was a member of the ethnic minority community targeted and who spoke the community language. Volunteers (other older members of the community or, often, siblings of children in the programme) worked with families to record, transcribe and translate stories from the community language and to produce from them a range of bilingual reading materials for children in primary school, appropriate to a range of ages. The second stage of the programme involved adult family members working with children in school on shared reading activities, using the story materials produced.

Intended outcomes

To achieve the aims; to produce a range of bilingual reading materials for children of primary school age; to involve refugee parents from this community in ESOL classes to improve communication skills in English; to increase parents' awareness of and involvement in children's experiences in school and the ways in which they might support their children's language and literacy development in English and in the community language.

Programmes 15 & 16

Background

These two programmes were located in primary schools in a city in South Wales. They were both co-ordinated by an adult basic education tutor based in the city's Job Review Unit which was part of the area's community education provision. The two programmes funded by the Basic Skills Agency as part of the small grants initiative were part of a larger development of fourteen family literacy programmes in the area. Provision for all these programmes was co-ordinated by the Job Review Unit.

Aims

(The two programmes shared the same aims, although they had different methodologies.)

To improve the oral communication of parents and children; to encourage parents to use everyday situations and events as stimuli for discussion; to enhance pre-reading, reading, pre-writing and writing skills of children; to provide opportunities for parents to recognise and value their existing skills; to provide opportunities for parents to improve their reading and writing; to give parents the opportunity to gain a qualification.

Methodology

Programme 15 intended to work with children, in Year 3/4 in a junior school, who were already part of a recovery programme operating for children with learning difficulties, particularly in literacy and communication. Parents of these children were recruited to participate in the family literacy programme. Programme 16 was based in the infant section of a primary school and intended to work with children in the reception class and their parents.

Both programmes offered separate sessions for children and parents and joint sessions. The programme content was related to Wordpower in order to provide opportunities for the accreditation of adult learning. In the two schools, family literacy sessions were held on one morning a week and lasted for three hours in total. Two hours were allocated for parents (and children) separately and one hour for joint work. The duration of each programme was 18 weeks over three school terms.

Intended outcomes

- 15 parents and 15 children to be recruited at each site over the period of the programme

- The children's progress to be assessed using National Curriculum levels of attainment

- The parents working towards Wordpower accreditation with pre and post-programme questionnaires to identify, for example: increased parent-child interaction; increased use of books and library facilities; increased oral fluency and confidence; increased ability to provide and access information and take part in discussion.

Programmes 17 & 18

Background

Programmes 17 and 18 were situated in the South-East of England. One programme was located in a first school serving a socially mixed area in a small town; the other was located in a Social Services Family Centre which served ten families on an estate on the fringes of an urban area. The first school which hosted programme 17 was not included in the original proposal, but became involved when one of the original partners was not able to participate. The two programmes were co-ordinated by an adult basic skills tutor based at the partner FE College.

Aims

To help parents communicate more effectively with their children and to communicate more effectively in the community.

Methodology

Programme 18, based at a Social Services' family centre, aimed to work with families selected by the centre manager from those served or on the waiting list. Families were to attend the centre for an extra half day a week to participate in the family literacy programme. Family literacy sessions were to be an integral part of the 'Family Programme' at the centre. The family literacy programme was to be staffed by centre staff (Social Services) and ABE staff from the partner FE college.

Intended Outcomes

- Improved communication skills for parents with their pre-school children

- Improved confidence and enjoyment for parents in assisting the development of their children

- Improved communication skills by parents within the community (for example with schools, agencies and medical bodies)

- Children benefiting from greater involvement in pre-reading, writing and language activities

- Children having the support of parents for pre-school requirements in language and behaviour.

Programme profile

Name of Programme _____

1. List Partners

1. Schools	Yes/No
2. Further Education Section Institutions (FESI)	Yes/No
3. TEC (Training & Enterprise Council)	Yes/No
4. Social Services	Yes/No
5. Libraries	Yes/No
6. Charities	Yes/No
7. Community Education Services	Yes/No
8. Special Government Initiatives	Yes/No
9. LEA	Yes/No
10. Local Businesses	Yes/No
11. Tenants' Association	Yes/No

2. Funding (Basic Skills Agency) _____

3. Funding (cumulative matching grants) _____

4. Pattern of Staffing

1. ABE Tutors (FE)   Yes/No
2. Youth and community workers   Yes/No
3. Visiting specialist tutor eg Red Cross, Dietician Yes/No
4. Community education workers (ABE)   Yes/No
5. School teachers   Yes/No
6. N Nurses/PPA worker   Yes/No
7. Supply cover/classroom support   Yes/No
8. Social services workers   Yes/No
9. Volunteers   Yes/No

5. Training for staff not qualified to teach ABE/ECE

1. None
2. Volunteers (1-1)
3. Professionals (1-1 and 1 to group)
4. Volunteers and Professionals (1-1 and 1 to group)

6. Aims

1. Followed ALBSU guidelines exactly (parent, child, joint)
2. Variations from ALBSU guidelines

7. Ways in which programmes vary from Basic Skills Agency model

1. Producing resources
2. Adult and joint sessions only
3. Adult sessions only

8. **Number of venues** _____

9. **Venue (adult)**

    1. School hall/library
    2. Classroom
    3. Room in school
    4. School library
    5. Other _____

    Venue (child)
    1. School hall/library
    2. Classroom
    3. Room in school
    4. Other _____

    Venue (joint)
    1. School hall/library
    2. Classroom
    3. Room in school
    4. Other _____

10. **Venue – suitability**

    (adult)   Suitable/Unsuitable
    (child)   Suitable/Unsuitable
    (joint)   Suitable/Unsuitable

11. Recruitment (audience targeted)

1. Focused on particular parents
2. Focused on particular children
3. General

12. Recruitment (main message)

1. Help child
2. Help parent with own skills
3. Both
4. Other _____

13. Recruitment (prime method)

1. Word of mouth
2. Printed adverts/letters/circulars
3. Initial meeting
4. Knocking on doors
5. Through other agencies (eg referrals of people at risk)

14. Recruitment (second method)

1. No second method
2. Word of mouth
3. Printed adverts/letters/circulars
4. Initial meeting
5. Knocking on doors
6. Through other agencies (eg referrals of people at risk)

15. About the course

Number of hours tuition offered (adult) _____

Number of hours tuition offered (children) _____

Number of hours tuition offered (joint) _____

Length of course in weeks (adult) _____

Length of course in weeks (children) _____

Length of course in weeks (joint) _____

Length of individual sessions in hours (adult) _____

Length of individual sessions in hours (children) _____

Length of individual sessions in hours (joint) _____

Main providers (adult) _____

Main providers (children) _____

Main providers (joint) _____

Curriculum content (adult)   literacy-orientated

interest-orientated

both literacy & interest orientated

Curriculum content (children)   literacy-orientated

interest-orientated

both literacy & interest orientated

Curriculum content (joint)   literacy-orientated

interest-orientated

both literacy & interest orientated

Participation in literacy/communication   high level

activities (adult)   low level

Participation in literacy/communication   high level

activities (children)   low level

Participation in literacy/communication   high level

activities (joint)   low level

16. Prime reason for not joining programme (non-participants)

1. Perceived as not relevant
2. Programme inconvenient/inaccessible
3. Not selected
4. Personal

17. BEFORE PROGRAMME

a. Similar work prior to programme (area level)

1. None
2. Some
3. Substantial

b. Similar work prior to programme (institutional level)

1. None
2. Some
3. Substantial

c. Similar work prior to programme (individual level)

1. None
2. Some
3. Substantial

18. AFTER PROGRAMME

a. (i). Continuation of programme (area level)

Yes / No / Not applicable

(ii). Continuation of programme (institutional level)

Yes / No

b. Where does the responsibility for continuation lie?

1. One partner
2. Joint partnership
3. Steering committee

c. Responsibility for future funding of continued programme?

1. Strategic planning locally (area)
2. Institutional developmental planning
3. Both

Adult participant profile

Name: _____

Programme: _____

1. **Biographical Information**

    Age: _____

    Sex: F / M

    Socio/Economic Status: Low / Not low

    Ethnicity: Caucasian
                                  South Asian
                                  East Asian
                                  Afro Caribbean

    First language: English
                                  Urdu
                                  Gujarati
                                  Punjabi
                                  Spanish
                                  Italian
                                  Bengali
                                  Somalian

Marital status (specify): _____

Children: Child 1   Child 2   Child 3   Child 4   Child 5
Age
Sex

2. Participants' education/qualifications

No formal education
No formal qualifications
CSE
GCSE or equivalent and above

3. Attitude/perceptions of their own schooling

Positive
Negative
Neutral

4. Prime reason for enrolment on course

Help child
Improve own basic skills
Social/education
Other _____

5. **Second reason for enrolment on course**

   No other reason
   Help child
   Improve own basic skills
   Social/education
   Other _____

6. **Attendance rates**

   _____ % of total _____ % possible

7. **Prime reason for non-attendance**

   Left area/left programme/moved into area/joined programme
   Parent ill
   Child ill
   Family matters
   Group dynamics
   Other _____

8. **Second reason for non-attendance**

   No other reason
   Parent ill
   Child ill
   Family matters
   Group dynamics
   Other _____

9. Perceived benefits/outcome (treat couples as individuals)

Adult

Confidence/Self Esteem

No change/negative

Participant reported positive change

Third party reported positive change

Corroborated positive change third party and participant

Competence (literacy)

No change/negative

Participant reported positive change

Third party reported positive change

Corroborated positive change third party and participant

Destination

Continued education/training

Employment

Both

Neither

Children

Confidence/Self Esteem	1st child	2nd child	3rd child	4th child	5th child
No change/negative					
Child reported positive change					
Third party reported positive change					
Corroborated positive change third party and participant					

Competence (literacy)	1st child	2nd child	3rd child	4th child	5th child
No change/negative					
Child reported positive change					
Third party reported positive change					
Corroborated positive change third party and participant					

Joint

Reported evidence of increase in:

Number of joint activities	Yes/No
Time spent with child at home	Yes/No
Shared literacy activities in the home	Yes/No
Involvement with child's curriculum	Yes/No

1. Individual Participants: Examples of Change

BACKGROUND	Case 1	Case 2	Case 3 (etc)
Personal Circumstances			
Own Education			
Reason for Attending			

2. Individual Participants: Examples of Change

CONSTRAINTS AND SUPPORTING CONDITIONS	Case 1	Case 2	Case 3 (etc)
Time			
Accessibility			
Other Aspects of Course Format			
Child Care			
Family Circumstances			
Personal Circumstances			
Local Circumstances			

3. Individual Participants: Examples of Change

TYPES OF CHANGE	Case 1		Case 2		Case 3 (etc)	
	Description	Evidence	Description	Evidence	Description	Evidence
Change in Own Learning						
Change in Child's Learning						
Change in terms of working with/relating to child						
Change in terms of relating to child's school experiences						

4. Individual Participants: Examples of Change

PROGRAMME DIMENSIONS	Programme Management	Working Collaboratively	Recruiting the Target Group	Implementing the Programme	Embedding the Programme
Promising					
Typical					
Less Useful					

Interview Schedule for Programme Administrators/Managers

Programme: .... Name of administrator: ....

Institution/Agency/Authority: .... Role in programme: ....

Date interviewed: .... Interviewer: ....

---

1. How did you come to participate in the Basic Skills Agency family literacy small grants programme?

   Probe
   - previous development work and involvement in other initiatives; how they heard about the small grants programme and the process of application for the grant. Whether the proposal was changed significantly in the process of negotiation with the Basic Skills Agency. Partnership arrangements/negotiations; how did each of the partners to bid come to be involved.

2. What would you say is different about family literacy from any other previous work which you have done in adult basic education/ community education/early childhood education/ work with parents?

   Probe:
   - personal/institutional notions/constructs of family literacy and relationship to previous work.

3. How were the staff (course providers/tutors/volunteers) recruited and prepared for the programme?

Probe

- whether staff chosen because of interest/expertise in this/related area; whether providers 'self-selected' to be involved

- previous experience/training/qualifications of staff/relationships (formal and informal) between staff involved in different aspects of the programme/from different partner agencies. Negotiation of ways of working with different providers

- further training/professional development offered, hoped to be offered for staff in programme (e.g. City & Guilds 9282).

4. Ideally, which target groups of parents/children were you aiming to recruit in the programme?

Probe

- how that group came to be targeted; needs analysis done before grant application; how was this done (i.e. systematically & rigorously or by 'best guessing' or previous experience with client groups)

- methods of recruitment and messages given; success in recruiting target group

- what kind (if any) baseline assessments of participants' literacy levels and competences were made on entry to the programme; descriptors used in assessing achievement.

5. What, for you, would mark success in this family literacy programme?

Probe

- in relation to parents' literacy/basic skills/educational achievement/confidence; in relation to children's literacy/confidence/integration into school practices/ joint activities

- future continuation of programme and progression of participants to other education/training/ employment

- emphasis on accreditation; what form and why chosen

- performance indicators of success in terms of partnership.

Interview Schedule for Programme Participants

Programme: .... Site: ....

Name of participant: .... Age: ....

Date interviewed: .... Interviewer: ....

1. How did you come to be on the course/programme?

Probe

- How did they get to know about it ?
- self-referral or referral by an agency e.g. social services.

2. Before you started what did you think the course/programme would be like?

Probe

- Whether course as experienced matches expectations
- Whether they knew that they would be working with their children.

3. Since you left school have you been on any other course/programme like this?

Probe

- for levels of post-16 education/vocational training/adult basic education
- if yes to above probe for details (e.g. how long ago; length of course/ training; formal qualifications or accreditation; degrees of success in terms of satisfaction and outcome).

4. How have you found this course/programme?

Probe

- degrees of ease/difficulty
- things enjoyed/found useful
- things found less enjoyable/useful
- for views on course content/method/interactions with tutor(s).

5. What benefits have you gained from the course so far/do you think you will gain in the future? (depends when in programme interview conducted)

Probe

- as individuals/adult learners/long and short-term
- as parents
- perceived benefits for children
- awareness of their children's literacy development & needs.

6. What would you like to gain from doing this?

Interview Schedule for Programme Providers/Tutors

Programme: .... Site: ....

Name of provider/tutor: .... Role in programme: ....

Date interviewed: .... Interviewer: ....

1. How did you come to be involved in this family literacy programme?

Probe

- how they heard of the initiative
- what motivated them to become involved/apply for the job/volunteer
- previous experience of similar initiatives/work/relationship to other work/post.

2. How would you describe your role in this particular programme?

3. From your point of view, what do you think is the most important thing you do on this course/programme?

Probe

- ways in which participants are helped with their own literacy/basic education/ their children's literacy
- what they think the parent participants want to get out of course/programme (ask for more details/specific examples of statements such as 'being more confident'; what would parents be able to do, having that confidence that they could not do before)
- for perceptions of longer-term benefits (to community; to participants' personal development; to children's schooling).

4. Where do you see involvement in this programme leading? (Personally/for agency or institution; what have you gained from involvement in this programme?)

Probe

- expectations/ambitions for programme
- institutional/agency support and constraints for future work.